The Cambridge Introduction to
Samuel Taylor Coleridge

Author of 'The Rime of the Ancient Mariner', 'Kubla Khan' and
'Christabel', and co-author with Wordsworth of *Lyrical Ballads* in 1798,
Samuel Taylor Coleridge was one of the great writers and thinkers of the
Romantic revolution. This innovative Introduction discusses his interest
in language and his extraordinary private notebooks, as well as his
poems, his literary criticism and his biography. John Worthen presents a
range of readings of Coleridge's work, along with biographical context
and historical background. Discussion of Coleridge's notebooks
alongside his poems illuminates this rich material and finds it a way into
his creativity. Readers are invited to see Coleridge as an immensely
self-aware, witty and charismatic writer who, although damaged by an
opium habit, responded to and in his turn influenced the literary,
political, religious and scientific thinking of his time.

JOHN WORTHEN is Professor Emeritus at the University of Nottingham.
He is the author of, among other books, *The Gang: Coleridge, the
Hutchinsons and the Wordsworths in 1802* (2001) and *T. S. Eliot: A Short
Biography* (2010).

The Cambridge Introduction to
Samuel Taylor Coleridge

JOHN WORTHEN

CAMBRIDGE
UNIVERSITY PRESS

CAMBRIDGE UNIVERSITY PRESS
Cambridge, New York, Melbourne, Madrid, Cape Town, Singapore,
São Paulo, Delhi, Dubai, Tokyo, Mexico City

Cambridge University Press
The Edinburgh Building, Cambridge CB2 8RU, UK

Published in the United States of America by Cambridge University Press, New York

www.cambridge.org
Information on this title: www.cambridge.org/9780521746434

© John Worthen 2010

First published 2010

Printed in the United Kingdom at the University Press, Cambridge

A catalogue record for this publication is available from the British Library

ISBN 978-0-521-76282-3 Hardback
ISBN 978-0-521-74643-4 Paperback

Contents

Illustrations

Preface

Down to the middle of the twentieth century, it was as a tragic, procrastinating, marvellous failure that Samuel Taylor Coleridge was most easily perceived. His great enemy the writer William Hazlitt had helped cement Coleridge's reputation as the ridiculously unproductive author of a few famous poems, the rambling prose book *Biographia Literaria* and a couple of religious polemics – nothing else surviving of him save memories of his irrepressible talk.

Today, seeing his collected works stretching out on library shelves in fifty volumes, readers are less likely to assume that he failed to write much. The twenty-first century has not only judged Coleridge to be the author of some great poetry and prose ('Kubla Khan', 'The Rime of the Ancient Mariner', 'Christabel', *Biographia Literaria*, for sure) but has come to view him and his poetry as iconic. The 'person from Porlock' who interrupted the writing of 'Kubla Khan' is a figure of mythic dimension, 'The Ancient Mariner' can today be found in many places and forms (illustrations by Gustave Doré, a song by Iron Maiden, a film by Raul daSilva, a gift shop in San Diego), while everywhere on the web are versions of a haunting Coleridge notebook entry: 'If a man could pass thro' Paradise in a Dream, & have a flower presented to him as a pledge that his Soul had really been there, & found that flower in his hand when he awoke – Aye! and what then?'[1] His contemporaries thought of Coleridge as a metaphysician (baffling or illuminating according to their point of view), as a philosopher (influenced by the German writers Immanuel Kant and Friedrich Schelling before most English philosophers had even heard of them), as a writer about religion and as the greatest talker of his age. Today, we are more interested in him as a poet, as an opium experimenter, as someone caught up in revolutionary politics, and in particular as a writer who described what he called 'the Flux and Reflux of my Mind within itself'.[2]

I present here a range of readings of Coleridge's work, along with some biographical context and historical background, but concentrating upon his own language and writing. I look at a number of his poems beside the famous ones, but also stress the range of his achievements; he himself was aware of 'a distracting Manifoldness'[3] in what he did. I explore areas where most readers will not venture without a guide, in particular the mixture of observation, quotation, dream material, philosophy and self-reflection in the 'undiscovered treasure'[4] of Coleridge's notebooks. There are also chapters on his poetry, his criticism and on his language.

It is certainly appropriate that he was the first person ever recorded using the word 'psychologically'; his intelligence as a psychologist feels entirely modern. His attempts to describe his own processes of apprehension, realisation and memory were at the heart of his achievement as a writer. He insisted, for example, on 'The dependence of ideas, consequently of Memory, &c on states of bodily or mental *Feeling*'; to him, body and soul were as inseparably linked as ideas and feelings, and as a writer he did his best to demonstrate it. He would, for example, question 'what is so constantly affirmed, that there is no Sex in Souls' and would answer 'I doubt it – I doubt it exceedingly'.[5] How could one be oneself and not in some way be one's own body? Such clarity and independence of thinking appeared not just in his notebooks and letters but in almost everything he wrote; it would doubtless have appeared in the novel he often considered writing, and to which in December 1815 he gave the title *Men and Women, a Novel.*[6]

After he became addicted to opium in the late 1790s, Coleridge's working life changed for ever. By virtue of an excellent memory and considerable help from others, however, he was able to write compellingly and at times superbly. He amazed even those who knew him well with his creativity in adversity, as when he proved able to write a whole number (6,500 words or more) of his newspaper *The Friend* 'in two days'.[7] Even at his worst he was possessed of a 'sense of responsibility to my own mind'[8] and it is often in his unfinished and fragmentary writings (poems, letters, notebooks, shorter works, marginalia in other people's books and uncompleted projects) that modern readers find him most powerful. This *Introduction to Samuel Taylor Coleridge* aims to suggest how appealingly and brilliantly he wrote, and to recommend further reading in the huge range of work he produced.

Acknowledgements

I am very grateful to Dr Linda Bree for giving me the opportunity to write this book and for her advice and help. Anne Serafin and Jim O'Hare lovingly initiated a huge number of improvements; Steven Vine read a draft and commented most helpfully. Hilary Hillier made detailed notes for me. Sue Wilson was her admirably savage self and provoked many clarifications; Peter Preston talked to me wisely. David Ellis read the final draft and made some valuable suggestions. Simon Collins made a beautiful job of the cover illustration.

Like everyone working on Coleridge, I am indebted to the Bollingen editions of Coleridge's Notebooks and Works.

Abbreviations

Works by Coleridge

CL   *Collected Letters of Samuel Taylor Coleridge*, ed. Earl Leslie Griggs, 6 vols. (Oxford and New York: Oxford University Press, 1956–71)

CN   *The Notebooks of Samuel Taylor Coleridge*, ed. Kathleen Coburn *et al.*, 5 vols. (New York, Princeton and London: Princeton University Press and Routledge, 1957–2002)

Bollingen edition of Coleridge's Works

All London and Princeton: Princeton University Press.

AR   *Aids to Reflection*, ed. John Beer (1993)

BL   *Biographia Literaria*, ed. James Engell and W. Jackson Bate, 2 vols. (1982)

C&S   *On the Constitution of the Church and State*, ed. John Colmer (1976)

CM   *Marginalia*, ed. George Whalley and H. J. Jackson, 6 vols. (1980–2001)

CPI   *Poetical Works I*, ed. J. C. C. Mays, 2 vols. (2001)

CPII   *Poetical Works II*, ed. J. C. C. Mays, 2 vols. (2001)

CPIII   *Poetical Works III*, ed. J. C. C. Mays, 2 vols. (2001)

EHT   *Essays on His Times in 'The Morning Post' and 'The Courier'*, ed. David V. Erdman, 3 vols. (1978)

Friend   *The Friend*, ed. Barbara E. Rooke, 2 vols. (1969)

L1795   *Lectures 1795: On Politics and Religion*, ed. Lewis Patton and Peter Mann (1971)

LL   *Lectures 1808–1819: On Literature*, ed. R. A. Foakes, 2 vols. (1987)

LPhil   *Lectures 1818–1819: On the History of Philosophy*, ed. J. R. de J. Jackson, 2 vols. (2000)

Logic   *Logic*, ed. J. R. de J. Jackson (1981)

LS   *Lay Sermons*, ed. R. J. White (1972)
OM   *Opus Maximum*, ed. Thomas McFarland (2002)
SWF   *Shorter Works and Fragments*, ed. H. J. Jackson and J. R. de J. Jackson, 2 vols. (1995)
TT   *Table Talk*, ed. Carl R. Woodring, 2 vols. (1990)
Watchman   *The Watchman*, ed. Lewis Patton (1970)

Other works

LW ii. 1   *The Letters of William and Dorothy Wordsworth: The Middle Years*, vol. ii, part 1, 1806–1811, ed. E. de Selincourt and Mary Moorman (Oxford: Oxford University Press, 1969)
OED   *Oxford English Dictionary*, second edition, CD-ROM Version 3.1 (Oxford: Oxford University Press, 2004, 2005)
PW   *The Prose Works of William Wordsworth*, ed. W. J. B. Owen and J. W. Smyser, 3 vols. (Oxford: Clarendon Press, 1974)

Chapter 1

Early life and contexts: 1772–1802

Samuel Taylor Coleridge was born in the small town of Ottery St Mary in Devon in 1772, the youngest son of a Church of England clergyman who was also a grammar school headmaster. His father was a scholarly man who wrote several books, including a Latin grammar; his mother was a capable organiser determined that her children should do well in the world. By the age of three, the boy was reading on his own; early and late he took every opportunity to read and to tell others about what he had read. By the age of six, he had discovered that at Ottery Fair the old books were 'formidable Rivals to Gilt Gingerbread' and had read among other works a volume of the *Arabian Nights* three times (*CN* v. 5829, *CL* i. 347, *Friend* i. 148). His whole future life depended upon this early initiation into the pleasures of reading; he lost himself in books, and nothing else would ever be quite so interesting. Later in life he described the technique of speed-reading he developed when young: 'stereotype-wise by whole pages at a glance: as if my eyes & brain had been a claud Lorrain Mirror, or a Camera Obscura' (*CM* iv. 336–7).[1] He did outstandingly at school.

He later became aware, however, of how odd his childhood had been. He had been the youngest of ten and had grown up (he believed) the favourite child of his parents, but was disliked and bullied by his brother Frank, so felt 'forced to be by myself' (*CN* ii. 2647). His constant reading meant that 'I never played except by myself, and then only acting over what I had been reading or fancying', while he developed 'none of the Child's Habits – I never thought as a Child; never had the language of a Child' (*CN* v. 6675). Being 'accustomed only to the conversation of grown persons', he grew 'arrogant, & conceited'.[2] Looking back, he believed 'I have always been preyed on by some Dread . . . from fear of Pain, or Shame' (*CN* ii. 2398); what drove a child like himself to religion and philosophy, he thought, was a sense of 'darkness felt in the day-light' (*SWF* i. 695).

In 1782, however, his father died, and his mother sent him as a boarder to Christ's Hospital school in London (orphans of the clergy were frequently sent there: but he was not an orphan). He lived the life of a city child in London, and loathed it: 'Deprest, moping, friendless' and constantly hungry (*CN* v. 6675). He never forgot the arbitrary punishments, Geography 'so sedulously cuffed into my Ears', for example (*CN* ii. 2015); he never forgave his mother. He would claim in 1804 that 'I was hardly used from infancy to Boyhood; & from Boyhood to Youth, MOST cruelly' (*CL* ii. 1053). He reckoned that his sleep disturbances were a consequence of his early life: 'Sleep a pande-monium of all the shames & miseries of the past Life from early childhood all huddled together, & bronzed [i.e. made unfeeling, hardened] with one stormy Light of Terror & Self-torture' (*CN* ii. 2091). His reaction, early and late, was to withdraw into himself, 'to crumple myself up in a sunny Corner, and read, read, read . . . with eyes closed to every object of *present* sense' (*CN* v. 6675).

He grew up a man who, in spite of his intelligence, astonishing memory, exemplary learning and great sophistication of thought, all his life remained '*a Boy*, as it were'; to his brother George he would confess how sad he was to have 'roam'd through life / Still most a Stranger' (*CN* iii. 3322, *CPI* i. 327). His constant search for figures who would sympathise with him was one indication of this; another was his alarming capacity for irresponsibility and evasion.

The least beloved

He also grew up feeling that he had lacked love all his life, and much of his subsequent experience was marked by attempts to be loved, liked and accepted. By 1793 he was rather hopelessly in love with Mary Evans, the sister of a school friend (he was also going to prostitutes); in 1795 he married Sarah Fricker, unhappily; in 1801 he fell in love catastrophically with Sara Hutchinson; in 1805, in Sicily, he was almost seduced by Cecilia Bertozzi. 'To be beloved is all, I need' (*CL* iv. 740) was how he summed himself up, but complained in 1808 how 'never, never, have I met with any Being who . . . loved *me* better than any one' (*CN* iii. 3442). 'No one on earth has ever LOVED me' was his anguished cry in 1810; in 1817, he would reiterate miserably how 'of all men known to me I am the least beloved' (*CN* III. 4006, *CL* IV. 740). He deeply envied those who *were* loved – for example, his friend William Wordsworth, 'happy in a sense undreamt of by the World' because of his marriage to Mary Hutchinson. Coleridge believed he had experienced just the opposite: 'so likewise do *they* most pine under the want of sympathy & [?loveliness/liveliness] and to them to be miserable in this is to be miserable in all' (*CN* III. 3648).

Unitarian

At Cambridge University from 1791, his prize-winning Greek ode on the slave trade was read at Commencement in July 1792; but the following year he failed to win the Craven Scholarship, which would have ensured him a career in the University or the Church. He had however gained entry into a circle of young radical thinkers who, having originally been excited by the French Revolution of 1789, were now troubled by the increasingly repressive regime in England. In 1792 there had been a Royal Proclamation against Seditious Writings and Publications, which ensured that republican writing like Tom Paine's *Rights of Man* would be suppressed.

It was not an accident that the group Coleridge fell in with, at Cambridge, were Unitarians; Unitarianism (the faith which affirms the unipersonality of the Godhead and denies the Trinity), like other nonconformist faiths, had a long tradition of radicalism in politics. Coleridge was (crucially) converted to Unitarianism; its religion offered yet another way for him to detach himself from his Church of England family, and – with his ability to read quickly, speak loquaciously and spend a vast amount of energy on what excited him – within a short while he had been thoroughly radicalised, to become what he later called 'a sharer in the general vortex' (*Friend* II. 146). It became an article of his belief that he had a natural antagonism to '*Gentility*' and he boasted of having been born 'a genuine Sans culotte, my veins uncontaminated with one drop of gentility'; he blessed his situation of 'being & *having been, Poor*!' (*CL* II. 881, I. 303, II. 750). Eight years later, Coleridge would suggest that Unitarianism was the proper religion for a man 'whose Reason would make him an Atheist but whose Heart and Common sense will not permit him to be so' (*CN* II. 2448); a keen insight into himself when young.

In May 1793 Coleridge was using his talent for eloquent interjection in the public hearings concerning a young Fellow of his own Cambridge college, William Frend. Frend had become a Unitarian, and had written in favour of non-Anglicans being allowed to enter the professions and hold Government appointments; University dons were currently required to subscribe to the thirty-nine Articles of the Church of England. Expelled from his fellowship for his beliefs, Frend had appealed to the University Senate; Coleridge joined other students in the public gallery to cheer and heckle, and was nearly seized by the University Proctor who came to arrest the most voluble of the protestors. At this stage, Coleridge considered a career as a Unitarian minister; his powerful belief in 'democratic principles' was entirely contemporary but in his case religiously based too. 'Christianity', he insisted, 'teaches in the most explicit terms the rights of Man'; 'it commands it's disciples to go every where . . . to preach these rights' (*CL* i. 282).[3]

By the autumn of 1793, however, extravagant living, alcohol and doing no work ('I became a proverb to the University for Idleness' – *CL* i. 67) had combined with his inability to handle money successfully. He ran up debts of some £150, but did not dare discuss the matter with his brothers, who were responsible for his finances. In a way that in retrospect seems characteristic, in a 'chaos of thoughts and feelings' (*CL* v. 84) he ran away from his problems; finding himself in a brothel may have provoked his decision. There was a tradition in his family of military service, of the kind in which boys entered the army as cadets, eventually to become officers (during his teens, his brothers had hoped to enlist him as a cadet). In accordance with his *sans culotte* sympathies, however, Coleridge went to London and signed up as a private (naming himself Silas Tomkyn Comberbache – still S.T.C.) in the 15th Light Dragoons; a crazy choice, as he could not even ride. It took further money to buy him out six months later. He went back to Cambridge in April 1794 but at Christmas left without a degree.

Pantisocrat and democrat

The reason he left was simple; he believed he had found a project and way of life for which a degree was superfluous. In mid June 1794 he had met the Oxford student and writer Robert Southey and they had jointly developed a utopian plan for an ideal society (which they called a 'Pantisocracy', meaning a community in which all are equal and all rule) to be established on the banks of the Susquehanna River in Pennsylvania, where the radical philosopher and scientist Joseph Priestley had been forced into exile. The idea consumed both men for months: 'America really inspired Hope, & I became an exalted Being' (*CN* ii. 2398), Coleridge commented. He later enviously recalled the days 'while I had yet Hope and onward-looking Thoughts' (*CN* iii. 3654); together he and Southey dreamed 'of the System of no Property' (*CL* i. 90). Southey had given up his studies at Oxford in July; Coleridge followed him by abandoning Cambridge in December 1794 to take up residence at Bristol, to be near his friend.

This meant that he was extremely hard up. Like Southey, he gave public lectures in Bristol in the spring of 1795 to generate a little income; lectures and occasional publications were almost his only means of support. What he *did* produce was often nearly extempore; he wrote a 'Moral and Political Lecture', he claimed, between midnight and breakfast-time of the day he delivered it. Like all his surviving lectures it was radical in its calls for 'Equality', but besides preaching justice it scrupulously cautioned against the excesses of the French Revolution (*L1795* 6). The lecture 'On the Present War' also offered a very controlled kind of radicalism, but of a wonderfully eloquent and witty sort. Soldiers are seditiously defined as those who 'might MURDER with impunity' – only for Coleridge to add, in the Errata: 'Page 61, for murder read Fight for his King and Country' (*L1795* 70 n. 2).

In August 1795, however, Coleridge quarrelled badly with Southey. The latter had inherited money and property, and changed his opinions. Coleridge suspected that 'No man's Heart can wholly stand up against Property' (*CL* ii. 750), while Southey, for reasons still unclear, believed that Coleridge 'behaved wickedly'.[4] The Pantisocratic project was, anyhow, abandoned. Coleridge turned to two of the great contentious issues of the day in England, the parliamentary Treason and Sedition Bills against liberty of the press and liberty of speech; these had been introduced late in 1795 following an occasion when King George III himself had been shouted at by a crowd. Coleridge brought out another pamphlet in December 1795, summing up his charge against the so-called 'Gagging Bills': 'The first of these Bills is an attempt to assassinate the Liberty of the Press: the second, to smother the Liberty of Speech' (*L1795* 286).

A pattern was, however, emerging, in which Coleridge's need for friends, love and admiration led him into alliances founded on the strength of his feelings at a particular moment. Because of his eloquence and gift of language, he could be taken for someone deeply convinced of certain principles, when he was more deeply motivated by his attraction to – or rejection of – an individual or a group. Some people saw this. Charlotte, the wife of the tannery owner and democrat Tom Poole, for example, described Coleridge as a young man of 'democratick principles . . . entirely led away by the feelings of the moment' (*L1795* xxix). The young Coleridge certainly said things about politics and government that were extreme. Later in life, perhaps rightly, he denied having *been* extreme. He originally believed, optimistically, that people liberated from tyrannical authority would properly enjoy the 'rights of Man'; he came to believe that the job of authority (secular and religious) was to restrain people from misusing their rights.

In October 1795, he married Sarah Fricker, the sister of the woman whom Southey would marry at the start of November. Southey had maliciously insisted to Coleridge that, because of the 'marked attentions' and 'direct addresses' (*CN* III. 3648) which Coleridge had paid to Sarah, she had turned down two other potential husbands, so that he was now obliged to marry her. Coleridge, with his 'Quick sense of Honor' and dread of his own conscience, felt trapped; he married Sarah 'for honor & not for love!' (*CL* II. 1156) and by the spring of 1796 she was expecting their first child. Writing poetry and journalism seemed the only thing for Coleridge to do, while they lived as cheaply as possible in the country (first near Bristol, later at Nether Stowey in Somerset). They were, however, very poor; Coleridge later described the 'bare walls of his Garret' and the problem for a pregnant Sarah of having to live up '3 pairs of stairs' (*CN* III. 3561). They were rescued by various people; Poole organised £40 cash a year, and the young Bristol bookseller and publisher Joseph Cottle paid Coleridge for a volume of poems (London publishers had turned down the idea).

At this stage, Coleridge, though writing pamphlets and poetry like many another educated young man, had no particular plan or ambition to be a writer; and of all the careers which might have been recommended to him, writing for money would not have been one. If he had not still been a Unitarian, a career in the established Church would have been a natural recourse. However, a life as a Unitarian minister also seemed a real opportunity, and he spoke as a lay-preacher until 1798. Another natural ambition would have been a University fellowship but – again – his Unitarianism made that impossible.

In fact, as Byron realised, 'Coleridge might have been any thing.'[5] He was a convincing preacher and lecturer; more than once he planned to earn his living by teaching; as a writer he was astonishingly fluent; he would prove a brilliant political journalist. He also worked successfully as private secretary to Sir Alexander Ball, the governor of Malta, in 1804–5; his surviving official letters are models of concision and directness (*CL* II. 1150–6). As it was, the fact that in 1796 Cottle published his poems (and also paid his friends for a volume he shared with them) gave Coleridge a reputation which he continued to exploit, while the extent to which he was prepared to live off others shocked a man like Southey, who with some envy described Coleridge as 'one who has neither the feelings nor habits of honest independence, & who always indulges himself careless of consequences'.[6]

Journalist

Buoyed up, nevertheless, by his marriage, his lectures, his poems and his pamphlets, Coleridge planned to edit a newspaper which would further democratic principles, and in which he could also publish his poetry. *The Watchman* would be a mixture of political journalism, serious and funny, most of it lifted from other newspapers, along with parliamentary reports and characteristically Coleridgian commentary; it would be supported by subscribers in nonconformist circles (Coleridge went to the Midlands and the North in the spring of 1796 on a publicity campaign).

It was especially concerned with reporting serious miscarriages of justice, with attacking the slave trade, with the Treason and Convention Bills and, above all, with criticising the continuing war with France. Its poetry was, by the standards of contemporary newspapers, excellent; its jokes sometimes good ones, with Coleridge engaging, for example, in a comparison between the Church establishment and the solar system (Bishop Pretyman getting typecast as Venus). He also provided parodies of *Court News*: 'On Thursday the Queen had a drawing-room at St James's Palace, *and all that –*'.[7] Such a witticism in itself would have been enough to label him seditious.

A jocular if scholarly essay on fast days in the second issue, however – containing an epigraph from Isaiah: *Wherefore my Bowels shall sound like an Harp* – cost *The Watchman* pious subscribers when it could not afford to lose a single one. To avoid stamp duty it was being issued every eight days and was attempting to undercut other such newspapers by being priced at 4d, not 4½d. But it carried no advertisements, and to be a success would have needed to sell a large number of copies. Some people stopped subscribing because there was not enough poetry in it; 'a still larger number' stopped 'because it contained too much' (*Watchman* 374). Coleridge also found that he could not recover from his London distributor the money the paper was earning. Every issue turned out to be costing him money rather than bringing it in; he had no choice but to cut his losses and stop publication. He had occasion one morning to scold the servant girl Nanny about the quantities of paper she was using to lay the fire, only for her to reply 'la, Sir . . . why it is only "WATCHMEN"' (*BL* I. 187). Years later he recalled the 'near 100£' (*CL* VI. 1034) he lost. He had to rely on Poole to pay the printer's bill.

He had the clever person's ability to laugh at his own mistakes as a way of putting them behind him, and the comic lightness of his tone about his early democratic ventures – 'I have snapped my squeaking baby-trumpet of sedition' he later repeated to two older men, to impress them with his maturity

(*CL* I. 240, 397) – is not altogether to be trusted. *The Watchman* had created for him a reputation as a democrat, and as a result he was able to get work writing political journalism and political poetry in London newspapers. This is a side of Coleridge's work which is not taken with much seriousness today, but it was something to which he turned his skills over and over again. His prose at this date is in fact a good deal more promising than his poetic rants in poems like 'Religious Musings', which spends 420 lines doing little more than blow rhetorical trumpets. In consultation with Daniel Stuart, the editor of the *Morning Post* (and later of the *Courier*), Coleridge produced leading articles for the Whig opposition, pieces opposed to the Tory Prime Minister William Pitt and the conduct of the war against France.

To do such work successfully, however, he needed to be in London. The years 1798, 1799–1800, and 1801–2 were consequently marked by his spending periods of time in the capital with his work appearing in the *Morning Post*. His work culminated in a portrait of Pitt (19 March 1800) written (Coleridge claimed) in a single evening which was widely praised; it was the kind of psychological demolition of a public figure that feels intensely modern. It describes how Pitt had fatally learned the 'management of *words*', and argues that such an ability, 'though it destroys genius, will often create, and always foster, talent'. And Pitt's talent was for '*general phrases*'; for 'Jacobinism' in the following extract, in the twenty-first century we might read 'Terrorism': 'Press him to an *individual* fact of advantage to be derived from a war – and he answers, SECURITY! Call upon him to particularise a crime, and he exclaims – JACOBINISM! Abstractions defied by abstractions! Generalities by generalities!' But though Pitt is (only) talented, he is also terrifyingly single-minded; his whole track has been 'as curveless as the motion of a fascinated reptile!' (*EHT* I. 220, 223). Coleridge's essay on Napoleon as companion piece never materialised, in spite of a flurry of promises. The Pitt essay, however, remains a model of journalism both populist and searching.

Friend

Coleridge's eloquence and intelligence deeply impressed everyone he met; during his twenties he was especially attracted to men and groups who, like brothers, offered him companionship and secure advice. Such men were often older than himself (at school Thomas Middleton, later Tom Poole, the minister John Estlin, later still the poet William Wordsworth), or their experiences made them (like Southey) at least seem so. They offered him the kinds of stability and reassurance of which his quickness of mind, constant excitement with the new, eloquence and deftness with language sometimes left him bereft. His friendship with William and his sister Dorothy Wordsworth, in particular, helped him concentrate on his poetry, and between the autumn of 1797 and the summer of 1798 he wrote most of the poems for which he is still famous (discussed in chapter 2). Wordsworth was in many ways a moral rather than a literary model for Coleridge; slow where Coleridge was quick, plodding where Coleridge was facile, and (to begin with) absolutely unknown compared with Coleridge, whose journalism and 1796 poetry volume had brought him some reputation. But Wordsworth had been in France in 1790, 1791–2 and (perhaps) again in 1793; he had had long discussions in France with committed revolutionaries; he had seen the results of the Revolution and also experienced the threats of the Terror, circumstances of which Coleridge had only heard. Wordsworth was, if anything, a more convinced opponent of the French war and the British Government than Coleridge was, though his attempts in 1794 to help found a political journal, the *Philanthropist*, had come to nothing.

Wordsworth's own rebellion against his family, both politically and in his determination to be a poet, had also been deliberate and painstaking. By the middle 1790s he was carving out a kind of poetry writing, in simple language and either blank verse or ballad metres, which immediately caught Coleridge's attention; this was perhaps the language and writing of the democratic revolution Coleridge had been so interested in. It was also a way of getting away from the literary language Coleridge had so far deployed in energetic, at times horribly rhetorical, hymns to ideals (and idealists). Coleridge's prose had been limited to the production of short-lived journalism or even shorter-lived harangue, he had spent a vast amount of energy in speculations about an ideal community which had come to nothing and he had married the wrong person. Meanwhile Wordsworth had been experiencing revolution at first hand and quietly working his way into a truly revolutionary kind of poetry, while deciding about the right place to live and the proper companions for his life.

Wordsworth was exactly the kind of moral exemplum to whom Coleridge was attracted, while Coleridge was characterised by a huge ability to be lovable, as Wordsworth and Dorothy discovered as they fell under his spell. They found his 'Imagination winged with fire inspiriting and rejoicing' (*CL* II. 1103) – the words of his friend, the great chemist Humphry Davy – and his 'creative energy' was irresistible. As chapter 2 shows, Wordsworth was caught up in the development of all the ambitious new poetry that Coleridge embarked on between 1797 and 1802, while, for his part, Wordsworth found himself pressured into writing the kind of philosophical poetry in which Coleridge believed. Coleridge went to Germany with Wordsworth and Dorothy in 1799 and in 1800 he followed them to the Lake District, where he and Sarah and their children lived thenceforth.

Self-watcher

Coleridge had grown up with what he once most accurately called a 'self-watching subtilizing mind' (*CPI* I. 454). The self-watching quality could be paralysing, though at times it enabled him to enquire into and vividly describe his own mental and emotional processes. When for example a surgeon was attempting to extract a thorn from his ankle in 1801, he gained (he insisted) considerable insight into 'the exceedingly interesting & obscure subject of *Pain*': 'O! how I *watched* myself while the Lancet was at my Leg!' (*CL* II. 772). 'I so attentively watch my own Nature, that my worst Self-delusion is, a compleat Self-Knowledge' (*CL* II. 882). The only problem was that he did *not* communicate what (on that occasion) he learned about pain. His ambition to write about it faded; his potential understanding died with the pain.

The 'subtilizing' capacity was also in its own way inhibiting, as it offered him ever further ways of considering a subject; some of his later work, and certainly his later conversation and lecturing, consisted of little except subtle elaborations of what he had started to say. At its best, however, it could be an incomparable gift. Following a night of 'Dreams full of Grief & bitter weeping' in 1804, for example, he immediately worked his feelings into a kind of poetry:

> Oft in his sleep he wept, & waking found
> His Pillow cold beneath his Cheek with Tears,
> And found his Dreams
> (So faithful to the Past, or so prophetic)
> That when he thought of what had made him weep,
> He did not recollect it as a Dream,
> And spite of open eyes & the broad Sunshine
> The feverish Man perforce must weep again.
>
> (*CPI* I. 762–3)

He noted to himself: 'This in rhyme, & either greatly compressed or highly touched up'. But having written that down, he could set to and analyse his experience in prose:

> And now for the Metaphysics/In cases of violent weeping is there not always Pity mixed & predominant? – Do we not pity our past Selves? – And Pity has always pleasure as one of its component Parts. Whence derived? Whence augmented? Sympathy will often make a Sufferer weep /. Is not this always accompanied by Hope?　(*CN* II. 2018)

And so on, for another eleven lines.

His writing, however, like his life, seemed equally divided between the pleasure he took in very real things and his intellectual pursuit of meaning and understanding; although very alive to contemporary politics he was even more deeply rooted in the past (especially in the writing of the seventeenth century) and in particular in its ways of writing about man's relations with the divine. His reading had always been immense, in depth and quality; late in 1796 he told one of the most single-minded of the democrats, John Thelwall, that he thought he had 'read almost every thing' (*CL* I. 260). He was not exaggerating. He would range from the philosopher William Godwin's *Abbas* (1794) to Xenophon, from the *Eikon Basilike* (the 1649 apology for King Charles I) to Henry Fielding's *Tom Jones* (1749), from John Donne's *Sermons* (1640) to Alfred Tennyson's *Poems, Chiefly Lyrical* (1830). His ambitions went still further. He intended, when young, to be 'a tolerable Mathematician, I would thoroughly know Mechanics, Hydrostatics, Optics, and Astronomy, Botany, Metallurgy, Fossilism, Chemistry, Geology, Anatomy, Medicine – then the *mind of man* – then the *minds of men* – in all Travels, Voyages and Histories. So I would spend ten years' (*CL* I. 320–1). He had, however, a living to earn, and he went on hoping that somehow he could do so by being a reader and thinker who wrote.

Metaphysician and Kantian

His serious thinking became inseparable from his attempts to understand his own life history; in 1803 he would note: 'Seem to have made up my mind to write my metaphysical works, as *my Life*, & *in* my Life' (*CN* I. 1515). At times he used the word 'Metaphysics' simply to mean analytic or psychological think-ing into root causes: 'That branch of speculative inquiry which treats of the first principles of things' (*OED*). In his own time, though, someone fascinated by things unreal or imaginary would also be classed a 'metaphysician', and Coleridge would become notorious for being engaged in 'abstruse Researches' (*CL* II. 1007). Lord Byron was responsible for the two most memorable insults, in *Don Juan* (1818); one describing Juan turning 'without perceiving his condition, / Like Coleridge, into a metaphysician', the other pillorying Coleridge for 'Explaining metaphysics to the nation – / I wish he would explain his Explanation'.[8]

Coleridge, intelligent man as he was, and capable of a good deal of self-irony, recognised his own tendency to 'devote himself to abstract sciences', even to '*downright metaphysics*' (*CN* I. 1065, *CL* II. 814), as an escape from his problems. He knew how he needed 'to force myself out of metaphysical trains of thought' which, for example, ensured that his poetry – instead of being comparable to 'wild Ducks *shaping* their rapid flight' – turned into a kind of 'metaphysical Bustard' (the great bustard *Otis tarda*, Europe's largest bird; Coleridge imagined metaphysical poetry 'urging it's slow, heavy, laborious, earth-skimming Flight' – *CL* ii. 814). He did what he could to redress his tendency to find 'a metaphysical Solution' for everything; he insisted that real thinking could never be simply abstract but must 'instantly *tell* for something in the heart' (*CL* ii. 961). He would later insist on the 'naked flesh & Blood, Bone and Muscle' of his own 'individual faith' (*CN* ii. 5784) in Christianity. Belief, like thinking, had to involve the whole self; it was not just the activity of an abstract intellect.

He had grown up impressed by the English 'associationist' or 'Idealist' school, especially by the philosopher David Hartley, who had argued that ideas were acquired by experience and entered the mind via the senses; the mind then brought appropriate ideas together by associating them. Coleridge, however, became disenchanted with the mechanical nature of Hartley's system; and in his reading of Kant he found a new way of coping with the problem of how the mind acquires experience. He now insisted that our experiences of what the eighteenth-century philosopher George Bishop Berkeley called 'outness' are, actually, of 'constituents or modifications of our own minds', not experiences of the world itself (*CN* iii. 3605). The mind *makes* our experience out of the sense impressions it receives; things do not simply come to us, via the senses.

Coleridge, in the end, for religious rather than philosophical reasons, would downgrade the role of the senses completely, remarking in 1832 that 'The pith of my system is to make the Senses out of the Mind – not the mind from the Senses' (*TT* i. 312). But that was in the future. In the late 1790s he was still looking for a way out of associationism. It has, for example, been convincingly argued that – following the example of the man who became his patron in 1798, Tom Wedgwood, son of the potter Josiah Wedgwood – what at first glance look like random jottings in his notebooks were actually conscientious research into our experience of the world via sight and touch.[9] In 1800 Coleridge summed up his intellectual project as 'a metaphysical Investigation of the Laws, by which our Feelings form affinities with each other, with Ideas, & with words' (*CL* i. 656); a huge project, characteristically proto-scientific (laws to be investigated), linguistic, philosophical and psychological. It would indeed be hard to think of a branch of human experience which would not be covered by such research.

Early in 1798, increasingly anxious about how to earn his living, he had come very close to accepting the post of Unitarian minister in Shrewsbury, and was only saved from it by the magnificent promise of £75 a year for life from each of the Wedgwood brothers Tom and Josiah, to enable him to read, think and write without financial anxiety. For the grand metaphysical 'Investigation' looked like a life's work. The actual writing, however, was for the future; his job for the moment was 'to be always collecting materials' (*CN* I. 1646).

Opium user

Two years on, however, late in 1800, Coleridge was suffering various kinds of crisis; he was deep into a worrying period when his life appeared 'a Blank' (*CL* II. 945) to him. Like most of his contemporaries, he had occasionally used laudanum (opium in spirits) as a painkiller; 'an agonising eye infection' in the spring of 1796, for example, had made him take it for two weeks. But that had led to his using it for its 'seeming magic effects'[10] and he had discovered the 'ease & *spirits*' it could bring: 'what a spot of inchantment, a green spot of fountains, & flowers & trees, in the very heart of a waste of Sands!' (*CL* I. 250, 394). By 1800 his opium consumption was not just an occasional practice but had become an unstoppable habit; he may have copied Tom Wedgwood's doctor's prescription of a daily grain.

At the start of the nineteenth century, however, opium-taking was almost as normal and insignificant as drinking alcohol. Byron used opium, so did Shelley, so did Dorothy Wordsworth, so (most famously of all) did Thomas De Quincey, who discussed it in his *Confessions of an English Opium-Eater* in 1821. Not only did many people of all classes use laudanum as a painkiller, but doctors prescribed it freely. A thoughtful and responsible medical book of 1793 described 'large doses of Opium' as something that, medically, 'may be employed with great advantage and safety'.[11] Coleridge would not have been alone in being 'fully convinced . . . that to a person with a stomach and bowels like mine' (their state in fact dreadfully upset by his opium habit), 'if any stimulus is needful, Opium in the small quantities, I now take it, is incomparably better in every respect than Beer, Wine, Spirits, or any fermented Liquor – nay, far less pernicious than even Tea' (*CL* II. 884).

That was not self-deception. For the person who has developed an opium habit, opium will indeed be the only thing that soothes the tormented body. It was well known that those who used the drug sometimes went on to take too much, just as drinkers did, but 'addiction' (a word originally meaning simply 'devotion to a pursuit') simply did not exist as a concept, either medically or linguistically, even for a man as massively well informed as Coleridge. The word would not acquire a medical meaning until the 1880s, and to refer to Coleridge's 'drug-abuse' (as some commentators do) is unthinking.[12] It was users who first understood the nature of addiction, by trying to reduce their dose. When they suffered what De Quincey, for example, called 'the Pains of Opium', they meant withdrawal symptoms (which, again, they could not have understood as withdrawal symptoms; no medical account of such things seems to date before 1824). For years Coleridge assumed that his own opium use was under control, unlike that of a contemporary he caricatured as 'stupified with opium' (*CL* II. 910).

Coleridge suffered withdrawal symptoms over and over again from around 1800. Without opium, or with too little, he would experience boils, rheumatic knees and legs, ulcers in his mouth, swellings in his scrotum; the only thing that dealt with the pain and discomfort was some quantity of opiates, which helped with the symptoms but of course confirmed the addiction, and also led to 'digestion-deranging' stomach problems: 'life-wearying uneasiness of the lower Bowels', 'the endless Flatulence, the frightful constipation when the dead Filth *impales* the lower Gut' (*CN* v. 6611, 6620, II. 2091). If he cut back on the opium, his stomach might get better, but sooner or later the cycle of pains, swellings and stomach problems would recommence (e.g. *CL* II. 1029).

During his Scottish tour in October 1803, he attempted giving up completely, and experienced the cold turkey feared by every junkie – heart palpitations, irregular pulse, 'intolerable Restlessness & incipient Bewilderment' (*CL* III. 476–7) – to discover once again that the only thing that saved him was the drug. He believed himself to 'bear Pain with a woman's Fortitude' (*CL* II. 1019), meaning better than most men, but withdrawal was too much for him; he imagined he would commit suicide if he really stopped taking 'that poison' (*CM* III. 747). The drug which enabled him to 'borrow half an hour's comfortable sensation' both fuelled his craving and increased his symptoms; the relief he got was, in the end, 'repaid in pain at a 1000 percent interest' (*CN* II. 2839).

To others, however, the problem (as De Quincey, the first English writer publicly to confess to his opium habit, voiced it) seemed simply to be 'opium used in unexampled excess', and Southey agreed, denouncing Coleridge for 'excess in opium'.[13] The obvious solution seemed to be to take less; but that led to withdrawal symptoms for those who, without knowing it, were already addicted.

Words like 'habit' and 'practice' were commonly employed to describe use of the drug. And such words suggested that, as the use was 'only' a habit, users were also at liberty to abstain. De Quincey would end his book with the assertion that by 'a determined abstinence from opium', he had reduced his consumption to nothing: 'I triumphed'. The claim was untrue but constituted an excellent ending for his book, and he repeated it in the 1856 version. He would personally assure Coleridge 'in the most solemn manner' that he had given up opium completely.[14] In fact he continued to use it until his death in 1859.

Such statements actually did considerable damage to those who were, without knowing it, addicted. In spite of his great clarity of mind, Coleridge had no option but to believe that he was weak-willed (he was denounced as such by friends and enemies alike) for not renouncing something that he hated, that everyone knew damaged him and which proved a terrible financial burden (his habit would, at its worst, have cost him over £100 a year) as well as – at times – rendering him almost incapable of everyday life and work.

If some of the best of his early writing was of nightmare and dream, and the dreams were partly opium-induced, then it is tempting to conclude that opium at least helped him in that respect. I do not, however, think it contributed one iota to the success of any of his writings, not even to 'Kubla Khan'. After leading to some early rapturous experiences, the drug became simply and painfully necessary. 'Opium when not *absolutely* necessary always has disappointed, and altered imperfect Comfort into downright *distressful* sensations & wretchedness' (*CN* III. 3468), he would explain in 1809.

He had, however, always been a man who put things off, given the chance. 'My very virtues are of the slothful order' (*CL* I. 132) he had confessed back in 1794, when Cottle had discovered how little 'finger industry'[15] Coleridge possessed. The opium habit contributed massively to the way it was 'always a struggle with me to *execute*' and to his 'inveterate habit of Procrastination' (*CL* II. 759, II. 820); it led to awful damage to his career as a writer as well as to constant agonies of self-reproach and guilt. His patron Josiah Wedgwood believed he saw 'the wreck of genius . . . without a hope' (*Friend* II. 464). Coleridge, however, went on attempting to conceal his need for 'old Blacky, alias, Opium' from those he loved and admired, which led him into all kinds of lying and insincerity as well as to accusations from others of 'a total want of moral strength'.[16]

Lover

Another awful problem (rather than joy) was the fact that, nearly five years married, by the late summer of 1801 he was deeply in love with 'the infinitely beloved Darling' Sara Hutchinson,[17] the sister of Mary Hutchinson, whom Wordsworth would marry in 1802. For years Coleridge had been quarrelling with his wife; he now dedicated himself to his love for Sara. More than ever he felt the need of somebody to bring him the love he had always yearned for, to free him from his 'consciousness and impulsive Feeling' of 'Self-insufficiency', to bring him nearer to 'that Blessing which is most present & perpetual to my Fancy & Yearnings' (*CN* iv. 4730, i. 1601).

His declarations of love to Sara Hutchinson, however, made her ill. It was probably in February 1802 that she wrote him a 'heart-wringing Letter, that put Despair into my Heart, and not merely as a Lodger, I fear, but as a Tenant for Life', and in May 1802 a 'second letter' apparently confirmed her rejection of his love (*CN* ii. 1912, 3401 and n.). This did not curtail his devotion: 'I inevitably by some link or other return to you, or (say rather) bring some fuel of thought to the ceaseless Yearning for you at my Inmost, which like a steady fire attracts constantly the air which constantly feeds it' (*CN* iii. 3708). He knew how unreal such love was: 'in health and in sickness, in Joy and in sorrow, in presence and absence . . . I have LOVED so as I should feel no shame to describe to an Angel, and which as my experience makes me suspect – to an Angel alone would be intelligible' (*CN* iii. 4006). He struggled on, keeping his ideal as removed as he could from his feelings of failure and self-reproach.

Writer

By 1802 he still did not know what kind of a writer he ought to be, and the Wedgwood subsidy meant that – because he, his wife Sarah and the children seemed just able to survive on it financially, if he could supplement it with money from occasional journalism and poetry – he did not have to decide. He liked nothing better than sitting in his study reading and making notes for the great work of religious philosophy he believed he had it in him to produce. He was also terribly aware of the lack of practical application of such a project. Walking in the Lake District, he had been caught by the fantasy 'To wander & wander for ever & ever' (*CN* i. 948), and his intellectual pursuits were always in danger of becoming an endless wandering after potential understanding. There were always extra books to be read, further authorities to pursue. He habitually worked on numbers of projects at the same time: '50 subjects with all the ideas thereunto appertaining'. If obliged to do anything in particular, like write journalism for a deadline, he would find himself 'always doing something else' (*CL* ii. 759; *CN* i. 935, 1646). Less and less did creative work like poetry seem to mean anything, even to him. He would remark, in 1801, 'I confess, I have written nothing that I value myself *at all*' (*CL* ii. 762). More and more he castigated himself for indolence while thus driving himself deeper and deeper into depression.

The Wedgwood brothers were unhappy about his failure to develop the work that their subsidy was designed to facilitate, but the opium habit assisted in making it impossible for him. At times he produced admirable journalism for Stuart and the *Morning Post*, and was well paid for it, but he felt it was beneath him; and, anyway, to write for the newspapers except at intervals would have meant forfeiting the Wedgwood annuity, which was to assist him in not wasting his time writing journalism for money. He started to rely on money borrowed or given.

And he went on producing very little, in spite of constant good intentions. He had drafted the first part of his poem 'Christabel' in 1798, and attempted to finish it in 1800, but only managed a fragmentary second part; and though the plan he and the Wordsworths evolved was that he should publish it as a complete poem, and over the years he continued to promise himself and others a third part that would complete it (and even told people that he was working on it, that he had finished 1,300 or 1,400 lines of it, or had almost finished it) he never seems to have written a line more than the 639 lines which survive, which did not get into print until 1816. An occasional poem in a paper and an occasional piece of journalism would be the only public evidence of his continuing capacity as a writer until 1809.

Before he was thirty, in October 1802, Coleridge had demonstrated over and over again his huge talent as a writer but had also committed himself to a way of life that led to disaster after disaster, personal and professional, as well as saddling him with an 'habitual Haunting' (*CL* ii. 959) in his dreadful consciousness of the gap between what he had aimed at and what he was achieving. He felt 'withered, having the faculties & attainments, which I have' (*CL* ii. 984). And this in spite of the fact that he had already achieved a lasting legacy of writing in his poetry.

Chapter 2

Poetry

The years 1797–8 changed Coleridge's writing of poetry (indeed his whole subsequent life) for ever. Not only did he meet William Wordsworth, but he also started to write the poetry of dream, nightmare and vision, created in simple, everyday language, with striking rhythms and insistent, repeated rhymes. The strangest and most fantastic things resulted. Even such undervalued works as the incomplete prose poem 'The Wanderings of Cain', the unfinished ballads 'The Three Graves' and 'The Ballad of the Dark Ladiè', and the weird little 'Fire, Famine and Slaughter', have their moments of horrible power. In the last named, Famine announces a recent sighting: 'A baby beat its dying mother: / I had starved the one and was starving the other' (*CPI* i. 442).

To the same period belong the three poems for which Coleridge is still best known: 'The Ancient Mariner' (finished but constantly revised), 'Christabel' (clearly unfinished) and 'Kubla Khan' (which he declared unfinished); all three in different ways taking us imaginatively into the dark places of the mind, in particular into the experiences of power and of its loss in nightmare.

It was once traditional to ascribe such a development in Coleridge's poetry to his use of opium, but distinguishing what a subtle and well-stocked mind might be able to imagine with or without opiates is impossibly difficult, and attempting to be more precise (by, say, identifying the figure of Life-in-Death in 'The Ancient Mariner' with the bringer of opium nightmares[1]) is simply arbitrary.

Another reason for the development of the major poems has been eloquently advocated; 'slavery' has been a key word in Coleridge poetry criticism during the last forty years.[2] Coleridge did indeed win the Browne prize for a Greek Ode at Cambridge, his poem being entitled 'The unhappy fate of the slaves in the West Indian Islands'. Although slavery had been illegal in England since 1772, the transatlantic trade in slaves had continued; William Wilberforce had brought in a second bill to Parliament in 1791 in an attempt to stop the trade, but had been defeated. Wilberforce and his supporters were nevertheless still doing their best to mobilise public opinion on the subject. Coleridge's choice of subject had therefore been thoroughly topical. In adult life he became a friend of Thomas Clarkson, a great and outspoken opponent of the slave trade; in 1810 he would make lucid notes about the effects of slavery on society (*CN* III. 3774). In 'The Ancient Mariner', the rotting planks (as well as the skeletal ship containing 'Death' and 'Life-in-Death') might well have reminded readers of the hulks in which slaves were transported; the poem is thoroughly of its moment.

It has, however, been argued that it was Coleridge's political stance against slavery and against powerlessness which made for the crucial change in his great poetry. The Mariner has been described as a figure 'who owes his being to Coleridge's political disenchantment', who 'journeys beyond the limits of geographic knowledge' and 'discovers his own powerlessness'.[3] Such statements contain so much exaggeration, and so little reading of the poem, that they are valueless. The Mariner is powerless not because he has journeyed so far but because 'tutelary spirits' (i.e. those protective of creatures like the albatross) have decided to punish him.

Coleridge is certainly interested in powerlessness and its consequences (of political and other kinds). But power, be it Kubla's or Life-in-Death's or Geraldine's, fascinates him just as much; as he rather regretfully noted in 1810, 'So all is *power* – active presence' (*CN* III. 3774). An over-concentration on slavery and powerlessness has been responsible for some rather one-sided readings of Coleridge's major poetry. 'Christabel' has, for example, been turned into a poem dominated by the portrayal of Christabel's father, Sir Leoline, as a corrupt aristocrat subjecting his daughter to 'tyrannical rage'. If the poem is really no more than 'a radical critique of the chivalric code',[4] it has been turned from a thoroughly disturbing analysis of the power and insidiousness of evil (as Geraldine worms her way into Christabel's affections) into something dull and entirely predictable.

It seems rather more likely that Coleridge's fortunate encounter with Wordsworth (and the latter's role as a deeply admiring critic), his own range of reading and the fact that he had not yet developed his opium habit, combined to allow him both calm concentration on (and insight into) the political world he knew so well, and into the states of individuals whose condition fascinated him, and that his best poetry drew on both. It is tempting to suggest that this was the time when, psychologically, he was at his most secure and careless; still happily married, a proud father, enriched by friendships with the Wordsworths, the Lambs, Thelwall and Poole, and for the most part a victim neither of illness nor of self-pity – this was the time when he really *could* allow himself to articulate horror and helplessness, and to imagine the reality of malignant power. The horrors in his earlier poetry ('Ruin' sitting 'Nursing th'impatient earthquake', or the 'black-visag'd, red-eyed Fiend outstretch' in his 'Religious Musings' of 1796) had been comic monsters; literary-political, impeccably blank-versed, gesturing but uncreated. The new kinds of horror were those of deeply disturbing experiences.

The poetry of extreme states

It is worth reminding ourselves why a man such as Coleridge might in the 1790s have immersed himself in the poetry of extreme states when we know that he was a confirmed enemy of the contemporary vogue for 'gothic' romance.[5] There are at least two explanations. One was the reason he gave in 1817, as he looked back at the experiments he and Wordsworth had conducted nearly twenty years earlier. They had decided that there were two kinds of poetry; one as close 'to the truth of nature' as possible, the other given 'the interest of novelty by the modifying colours of imagination'. Coleridge himself, partly because of his deep interest in psychology, was attracted to the latter kind of poetry, to what he called 'persons and characters supernatural, or at least romantic' (*BL* ii. 5–6). Ever a man rooted in the eighteenth century, and a stickler for literal meanings, by 'supernatural' Coleridge meant 'above and beyond the natural'; 'extraordinary' would be a seriously close synonym.[6] The word as he used it had nothing necessarily to do with spirits or with other realms than the human. His attraction to supernatural experience and to the people caught up in it would 'transfer from our inward nature a human interest and a semblance of truth sufficient to procure for these shadows of imagination that willing suspension of disbelief for the moment, which constitutes poetic faith' (*BL* ii. 6). Coleridge thus immediately offered a reason why poetry that singled out such people and such feelings could nonetheless be 'real' to its readers. It would be true to 'the moment' while simultaneously appealing to 'our inward nature'; it would be psychologically true. Like the Mariner, Christabel undergoes supernatural *and* spirit experiences; we are brought to imagine them and realise them, and for that very reason we are powerfully recalled to the natural, which as readers we experience as if for the first time.

Coleridge's clear-sighted versions of horror (in particular the contrasts of power and helplessness, responsibility and guilt – all terribly natural things), which his poetry explored between 1797 and 1798, were insights he seems later to have realised were exceptional. As early as 1800 he would be more cautious about where he allowed himself to go, imaginatively and morally; he started by removing from 'The Ancient Mariner' some of its weirder and more frightening passages, and added to the poem the apologetic subtitle 'A Poet's Reverie'.[7] In 1803, in his poem 'The Pains of Sleep', he would be superbly articulate about what it felt like to be the victim of nightmares, but the poem itself would not take its readers very far into the nightmare experience. Nightmares in Coleridge's imaginative writing thereafter would be described, but not participated in. In his great years as a poet, however, exactly the opposite had been true.

The unfinished, the revised

The poems he did not finish in these early years, though he carefully preserved them, mostly remained as fragments. 'The Three Graves' ends with the note (in Latin) 'the rest of the poem was postponed until a future time' and then (in English) the Shakespearian reminder: 'To-morrow! and To-morrow! and To-morrow!' (*CPI* I. 349, 512). 'Kubla Khan' begins with a lengthy explanation of why it is only a fragment but also ends with a note in Greek ('I shall sing a sweeter song tomorrow') and the English commentary 'but the to-morrow is yet to come'. A preface to 'The Wanderings of Cain' offers its own explanation of why the piece is in prose and why a fragment; the preface to 'Christabel' simply states the dates of its two (unequal) sections.

The unfinished work is, nevertheless, in its own way a proof of a demand for authenticity; a demand that did not allow such work simply to be rounded off, as a work like 'Religious Musings' had (more than once) been rounded off. Poems of the kind Coleridge started to write in 1795 which he *did* finish, however, often found themselves subjected to years of serious revision, rewriting and re-focusing. Discussion of a well-known poem like 'The Eolian Harp' is made infinitely more complex by the way Coleridge changed it over and over again; in 1796, in 1803 and then again for the 1817 edition of his poems, when its most famous lines – 'O the one life within us and abroad / Which meets all motion and becomes its soul' (*CPI* i. 233) – were added at the last minute, so that they could only appear in the book's Errata. The initial version of 'This Lime Tree Bower my Prison', dating from 1797, fifty-five lines long, was supplanted by an extensively rewritten version more than twenty lines longer; the even better-known 'Frost at Midnight', of 1798, was heavily revised from an eighty-five-line original to a final poem of seventy-four lines, with a further eight lines being added, and then removed, along the way. Handwritten annotations surviving in printed copies of his own work demonstrate just how often he emended it. It is always worth going back to the earliest versions of Coleridge's poems before seeing what he later made of them.

The point is that we should never assume that the 'final' version of a poem represented what Coleridge had always been trying to achieve; he rewrote his poetry as carefully as he rewrote his early life. Part of his continuing fascination comes from observing the different selves he enacted at different times, and in tracing the way he regarded his own published writing as unstable – in process – almost to the same degree as his unfinished work.

'The Rime of the Ancient Mariner'

'The Ancient Mariner' is the only one of the four 'great poems' by Coleridge which could be appreciated by his contemporaries as a finished poem (though in two rather different versions). He laboured over its original composition concentratedly for months, as he was still in a condition to do in 1797–8, but he also went on revising it for the rest of his life. Like us, he knew how suggestive a work it was, and he saw new things in it all the time. According to Wordsworth in 1843, the poem had started from the idea of 'a crime' and a consequent 'spectral persecution' (*CPI* i. 366). Coleridge spent a good deal of time over the years trying to define more exactly the nature of the 'crime' which the Mariner commits and the nature of the 'spirits' who persecute him, but more explanation in such a case sometimes means less. Exactly why shooting an albatross with a crossbow should be *such* a crime was always going to be mysterious; as mysterious as why the Mariner shoots it in the first place, for which there is no explanation at all. 'I shot the albatross' is all he says (*CPI* i. 378). The killing seems just as inevitable as the dice game later played for the Mariner, in which he is won by the character in 1817 named as 'Life-in-Death', as opposed to just 'Death' (although from the start it was clear that 'she is far liker Death than he' – *CPI* i. 386–7).

> The naked Hulk alongside came
>   And the Twain were playing dice;
> 'The Game is done! I've won, I've won!'
>   Quoth she, and whistles thrice.
>
>   (*CPI* i. 386)

In the 1817 version then follows the terrifying conclusion, as if the whole earth were responding to her whistle:

> The Sun's rim dips; the stars rush out:
>   At one stride comes the dark . . .
>
>   (*CPI* i. 387)

And then, possessed by Death, the sailors die, in a way that reminds the Mariner very evocatively of his guilt:

> Their souls did from their bodies fly, –
>   They fled to bliss or woe;
> And every soul it pass'd me by
>   Like the whiz of my Cross-bow.
>
>   (*CPI* i. 388)

The simplicity of the poetry remains one of its greatest achievements. As William Empson remarked, it reads 'as if English had been evolved solely to write this one poem'.[8]

Why should the Mariner be so afflicted? The only answer can be that he simply is. This is how things happen in ballads and nightmares, and becoming the personal property of 'Life-in-Death' means that the Mariner will go on suffering horrors. The ship's crew accompanying the Mariner had originally applauded him for killing the bird 'That brought the fog and mist' and then (when they were becalmed) had excoriated him for killing the bird 'That made the breeze to blow'; they had disabled him by hanging the huge dead bird around his neck 'Instead of the Cross', as his own special cross that he now has to lug around.[9]

The point, however, seems to be that whereas sailors shooting birds (often for food) could be taken for granted,[10] shooting a bird that is trusting and familiar, that comes to the sailors' call and eats biscuit-worms, is wrong. The bird is oddly suggestive of a blessing bestowed, arriving 'an it were a Christian Soul', and in the onrush of the ballad it probably does not occur to us to ask whether killing such a bird should be judged criminal. It simply *is*; and the consequences work themselves out, as the Mariner is pursued by the forces he has unwittingly let loose, while 'Death', having won them, kills his four times fifty fellow sailors, who have done nothing wicked at all.[11]

But that is just how it is in nightmares. 'O let me be awake, my God!' (*CPI* I. 406) begs the Mariner. If 200 sailors are taken out, so be it; we are only really concerned with the central narrator, and with the awfulness of *his* nightmare experience, prisoner as he is of 'Life-in-Death':

> Alone, alone, all all alone
> Alone on the wide, wide sea.
>
> (*CPI* I. 390)

Deep down, the point is that the consequences of such a 'crime', and of 'spectral persecution', cannot be worked through or transcended. Just as there is no simple crime, there can never be any simple release. The vision of the rotting ocean, where 'slimy things did crawl with legs / Upon the slimy Sea' (*CPI* I. 380), is quite appalling; 'Life-in-Death', which not only permits such visions but encourages them, *is* worse than simple death, because to Coleridge's mind one is compelled to go on registering and recording the unbelievably awful things one sees and does, as he always faithfully did, and as he makes his Mariner do too.

The revenges of the 'tutelary spirits', once set in motion, simply operate. Just when we think the Mariner must after all have suffered enough and is being allowed to go home, a spirit quietly announces that 'the man hath penance done, / And penance more will do' (*CPI* I. 402), setting us up to expect Part VI and Part VII of the poem to continue the nightmare. Much of the middle of the poem is simply about the way the ship gets blown about or becalmed or (terrifyingly) moves again; actions entirely out of the power of the helpless central human figure.

The Mariner may finally be brought to survive the appalling voyage and an equally appalling homecoming, when (in the 1798 version), before the ship goes down 'like lead', the bodies of the sailors advance 'before the mast' – they feel exactly like a group of mutineers confronting the ship's master – and stand glaring at him with their right arms aflame:

> They lifted up their stiff right arms,
>   They held them strait and tight;
> And each right-arm burnt like a torch,
>   A torch that's borne upright.
> Their stony eye-balls glitter'd on
>   In the red and smoky light.
>
> (*CPI* I. 408)

Coleridge cut those lines in 1800. They feel intensely pagan, drawing as they do on the old superstition of the 'Hand of Glory' (when the flaming hands of the dead prevent movement by anyone who encounters them), but they also mark the final accusations of the murdered crew directed at the Mariner who has been responsible for their deaths. When the Mariner looks back at them, the burning, threatening corpses have been replaced by angelic figures who are not in the least threatening, and I suspect that Coleridge wanted to get those more reassuring figures into the poem rather sooner; hence the cut he instituted.

Nevertheless, 'Life-in-Death' has won the Mariner and holds on to him. The Mariner, although in one sense safe, is now condemned to wander and relive his story, which haunts all those who hear it, as he is haunted, and as we readers have now been haunted. The Mariner may offer the wedding-guest a good, sound moral about having now learned to love 'All things both great and small', because God 'made and loveth all' (*CPI* i. 418), and it has been claimed that through 'spiritual redemption' the Mariner 'finds his own spiritual home';[12] but it is very hard to square such a moral with what the poem has shown and made unforgettable (the intensely unlovable slimy creatures with legs, the monstrous pair of gamblers on the skeletal ship, the stony-eyeballed dead sailors with their arms aflame, the wolf which eats his own children, the ship that goes down like lead) or with the Mariner's continued obligation to tell his story and harrow his hearers. Such 'love' for 'All things both great and small' is a very tough sort of love. Drawing a child-like moral seems no more than the Mariner's way of coping.[13]

The wedding-guest's very different state of senseless shock (he is 'one that hath been stunn'd / And is of sense forlorn') and his subsequent state of mind − 'A sadder and a wiser man / He rose the morrow morn' (*CPI* i. 418; 'We are not told he slept'[14]) − suggest a richer response to the poem's disturbing experiences than the Mariner's moral could ever provide, or the Mariner himself might ever risk. Human beings, because they are the victims of their sensibilities, their emotions and their memories, as well as of their nightmares, can go through quite appalling experiences, which is something our everyday life often conveniently helps us ignore – until we encounter the poem which will not allow us to forget.

Coleridge himself was haunted by ideas of loneliness and loss; a year before writing his poem, he had feared to 'be again afloat on the wide sea unpiloted and unprovisioned' (*CL* i. 273). Not only did he continue to revise the finished poem but he regularly revisited it. In 1801, for example, when describing himself as 'an object of moral Disgust to my own Mind' (*CL* ii. 726), he would picture himself 'shipwrecked by storms of doubt, now mastless, rudderless, shattered, – pulling in the dead swell of a dark & windless Sea' (*CN* i. 932); a Mariner in a small boat uncertain of where he is going or what he might do, but obliged to explain himself. He also regularly quoted the poem to himself; as late as December 1827, for example ('a wicked whisper comes') and May 1828 ('at one stride comes the dark' – *CN* v. 5689, 5860).

'Christabel'

'Christabel', despite influencing Walter Scott and being known to Byron, was not published for nearly twenty years after it was written. Coleridge wrote Part I in Somerset in the spring of 1798, and – determined to finish it – worked immensely hard to produce Part II in the Lakes during the early autumn of 1800. But Part II remains unfinished, and he never wrote any more. The reason commonly given is Wordsworth's so-called 'rejection' of the poem for the second edition of *Lyrical Ballads* in October 1800; biographers and critics alike have graphically described the way that Coleridge's belief in himself as a poet was undermined, so that he never again wrote any significant poetry.

The evidence, however, does not stack up. Coleridge's great friend Charles Lamb, who had read the first part of the poem, did not believe that anything could be done to improve on it, and was very angry when he heard that Coleridge had written a second part (*CPI* i. 478). Furthermore, Wordsworth did not reject the poem; he and Dorothy deeply admired Parts I and II. However, they agreed with Coleridge that the poem (planned to grow another thousand words or so) was already far too big and far too complex for *Lyrical Ballads*, and would do much better published on its own when Coleridge had finished it. Coleridge was not undermined and within eighteen months was hard at work on one of his great works of poetry, the 'Letter' poem which led to 'Dejection: An Ode'.

The latter part of 1800, however, coincided with his deep dip into opium habituation; he did not manage to produce a single major independent publication between 1800 and 1813. 'Christabel' lived on in a kind of underground existence, talked about and repeated from friend to friend; a friend who had a manuscript showed it to Scott, whose 'Lay of the Last Minstrel' (1805) was influenced by it.

It also seems possible that, as with 'Kubla Khan', Coleridge realised that although he knew how the poem might have ended (he told James Gillman all about it twenty years later), the haunting and tantalising unfinished state of the poem allowed Geraldine – and her growing hold over Christabel – to be a great deal more worrying and powerful than would have been possible in any finished version. In Part I, all Geraldine *does* is undress and to some extent reveal herself:

> Beneath the Lamp the Lady bow'd,
> And slowly roll'd her eyes around,
> Then drawing in her Breath aloud,
> Like one that shudder'd, she unbound
> The Cincture from beneath her Breast:
> Her silken Robe and inner Vest
> Dropt to her feet, and fell in View,
> Behold! her Bosom and half her Side
> Are lean and old and foul of Hue –
> A Sight to dream of, not to tell!
> O shield her! shield sweet Christabel!
>
> (*CPI* i. 490–1)

– and then she enunciates the first of her spells:

> 'In the Touch of this Bosom there worketh a Spell,
> Which is Lord of thy Utterance, Christabel! . . . '
>
> (*CPI* i. 491)

The problem of explicit evil is already emerging, and if the poem had been taken to the end, what Coleridge later called Geraldine's 'witchery by daylight' (*TT* i. 410) would have had in some way to be both explained and defeated. In 1804, flashes of lightning seen in broad daylight sent Coleridge's mind straight back to his creation: 'the terror without the beauty. – A ghost by day time / Geraldine' (*CN* ii. 2207). Yet even to call her 'a ghost' reduces her; she would have been still further diminished if the poem had really drawn to a conclusion.

Fortunately the poem as we have it – especially what we now think of as Part I – remains mysterious. Motiveless malignity discovered out in the forest, in the person of Geraldine, apparently vulnerable, hospitably invited and welcomed into your own home, starting to operate upon your own father, starting to infect you yourself (Christabel finds herself hissing, snake-like, under Geraldine's influence); these are the things that make 'Christabel' powerful. Coleridge went on for years considering how he might continue it; friend after friend heard his plans (*CPI* i. 478–9). But it looks rather as if it had been Coleridge's intelligent inner monitor which had prevented him from taking Part II any further and finishing (i.e. spoiling) it. He had done enough to haunt generations of readers.

'Kubla Khan'

Almost everything about 'Kubla Khan' has become extraordinary: its hypnotic power, Byron's fascination with the line about 'woman wailing for her demon lover', its legendary status as a poem produced under the influence of opium, the way in which Coleridge invented the 'person from Porlock' to explain why the poem stopped where it did (if indeed it was not already complete). Coleridge even invented for it the simple word 'greenery', new to the English language.

It is instructive to see what he did to his prose source. He had been reading Samuel Purchas's *Purchas His Pilgrimage* (1617):

> *In Xamdu did Cublai Can* build a *stately* Palace, encompassing sixteene *miles* of plaine *ground with a wall*, wherein are *fertile* Meddowes, pleasant springs, delightfull Streames, and all sorts of beasts of chase and game, and in the middest thereof a sumptuous house of *pleasure*, which may be removed from place to place.   (*CPI* I. 511)

The poem (see Figure 1) starts:

> In Zannadù did Cubla Khan
> A Stately Pleasure-Dome decree
> > (*CPII* I. 676)

'A sunny Pleasure-Dome with Caves of Ice!' (*CPII* I. 677) exclaims the poem a little later, but Purchas describes no dome, no caves, no ice; above all, he conveys no special sense of power or control. And it is the poem's versions of power which make it so horribly entrancing.

First, there is the power of the Khan, whom Coleridge once referred to as 'the greatest Prince in Peoples, Cities, & Kingdoms that ever was in the World' (*CN* I. 1841), who has not just had made a sumptuous little movable garden house, as in Purchas, but a grand Pleasure-Dome constructed by 'decree' (a positively god-like act, consistent with his domination of the sacred river Alph[15]). There follows a sequence of images of power: the huge force of the geyser bursting from its chasm, not just shifting rocks but making them 'vault' and 'dance'; the noisy power of the river crashing into the ocean far below; the hypnotic power of the damsel with the dulcimer; the quiet power of the sunny Dome miraculously sustained on its caves of ice; finally the dangerous creative power of the poet-figure, who promises to take away your self-control:

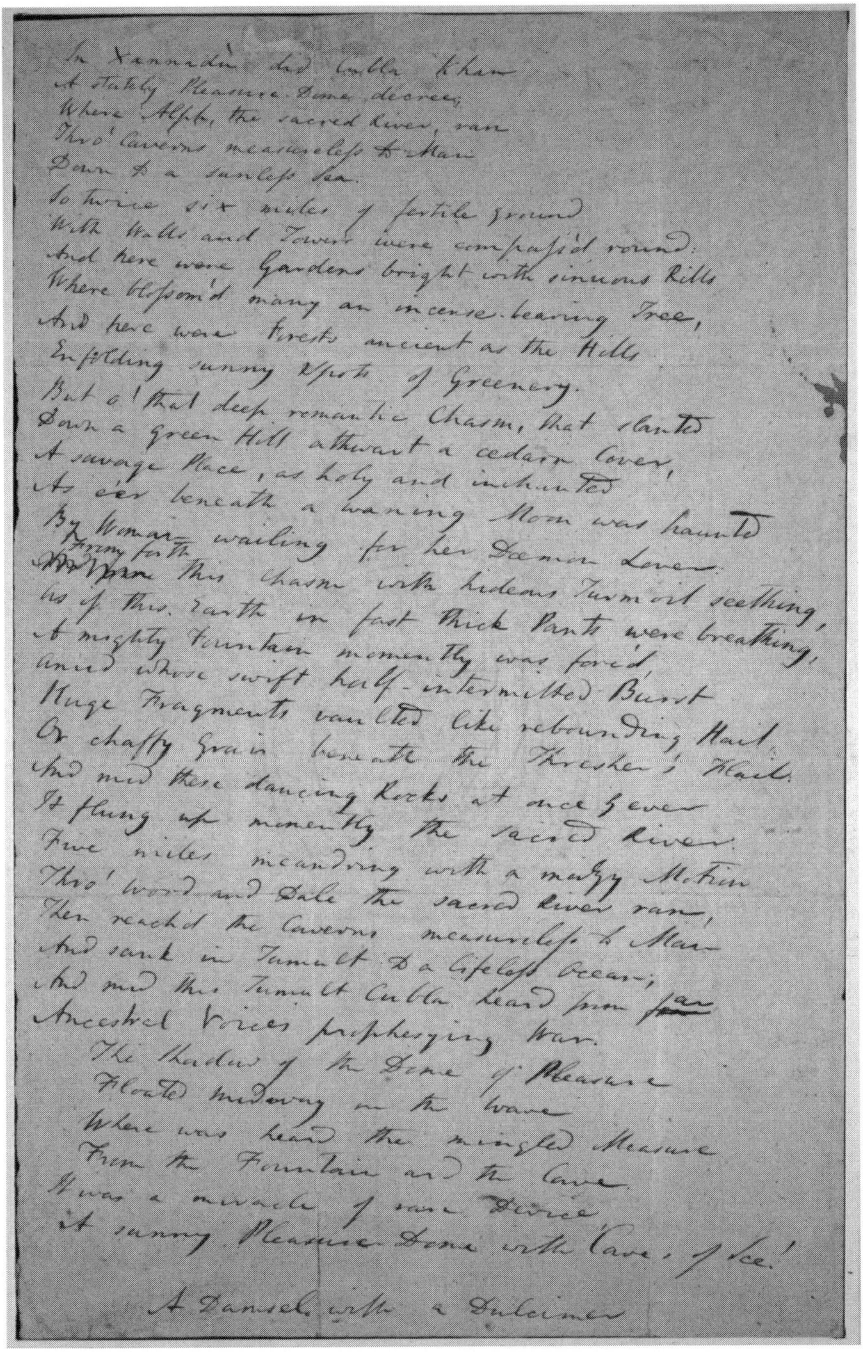
In Xannadù did Cubla Khan
A stately Pleasure-Dome decree;
Where Alph, the sacred River, ran
Thro' Caverns measureless to Man
Down to a sunless Sea.
So twice six miles of fertile ground
With Walls and Towers were compass'd round:
And here were Gardens bright with sinuous Rills
Where blossom'd many an incense-bearing Tree,
And here were Forests ancient as the Hills
Enfolding sunny Spots of Greenery.
But o! that deep romantic Chasm, that slanted
Down a green Hill athwart a cedarn Cover,
A savage Place, as holy and inchanted
As e'er beneath a waning Moon was haunted
By Woman wailing for her Dæmon Lover:
From forth this Chasm with hideous Turmoil seething,
As if this Earth in fast thick Pants were breathing,
A mighty Fountain momently was forc'd,
Amid whose swift half-intermitted Burst
Huge Fragments vaulted like rebounding Hail,
Or chaffy Grain beneath the Thresher's Flail:
And mid these dancing Rocks at once & ever
It flung up momently the sacred River.
Five miles meandring with a mazy Motion
Thro' wood and dale the sacred River ran,
Then reach'd the Caverns measureless to Man
And sank in Tumult to a lifeless Ocean;
And mid this Tumult Cubla heard from far
Ancestral Voices prophesying War.
The Shadow of the Dome of Pleasure
Floated midway on the Wave
Where was heard the mingled Measure
From the Fountain and the Cave.
It was a miracle of rare Device
A sunny Pleasure-Dome with Caves of Ice!
A Damsel with a Dulcimer

Figure 1 'Kubla Khan' (British Library Add. MS 50, 847 f.1).

> And all, who heard, should see them there,
> And all should cry, Beware! Beware!
> His flashing Eyes! his floating Hair!
> Weave a circle round him thrice,
> And close your Eyes in holy Dread:
> For He on Honey-dew hath fed
> And drank the Milk of Paradise. –
>
> (*CPII* i. 677)

Purchas gave Coleridge no clue for any of that. 'Kubla Khan' is so well known that it is easy to forget or ignore its moments of horror, as when we read of the sacred river sinking

> in Tumult to a lifeless Ocean:
> And mid this Tumult Cubla heard from far
> Ancestral Voices prophesying War.
>
> (*CPII* i. 676)

There is, too, the revelation that the entranced poet-figure of the last section himself might be able, if influenced sufficiently by the damsel singing about 'Mount Amora', to 'build' the dome and the caves.

We realise that, as readers, we are in the middle of a poem where exactly that is being been done for us and to us. Especially to us. We too have been entranced, hypnotised by rhyme and rhythm and suggestion, as the poet-figure is entranced ('His flashing Eyes! his floating Hair!'), and the dome and caves are simultaneously a vision and very actual as the poetry make us feel them.

We know too how they supply a vivid image of the mind itself: apparently sunny, fertile, broad and spacious on the top, with trees and brooks and houses, blossoms and incense, despotically ruled by one who feels himself supremely powerful; yet with all kinds of currents and caves and fountains further down, along with a great chasm slanting down the hill, a tremendous fountain making rocks bounce, and eventually dull, sullen seas strangely connected with each other, far away below. The poet-figure may drink the milk of paradise but it certainly does not succeed in taming him. Just the opposite; his power over your mind now needs, somehow, to be controlled ('Weave a circle round him thrice'). You had better close your eyes too, if he is not to take you over, as the Mariner takes over the wedding-guest. Kubla Khan was a monstrous figure of despotic control but the poem is very clear in showing, too, how 'That . . . is what an artist is like'.[16]

To Coleridge's equally entranced friends, the poem was unforgettable. When Dorothy Wordsworth went to the fountain in the market place at Brunswick on 6 October 1798, she casually referred to her water can by its pet name of *Kubla*, incidentally revealing how both she – and Coleridge, who would have repeated the name to her and her brother – pronounced 'Khan'.[17] In every sense she carried the idea with her, even on a domestic errand. Once heard, never forgotten.

'Conversation' poems

Coleridge's so-called 'Conversation' poems of the middle and late 1790s have always attracted an audience; the natural world speaking to the poet prepared to listen, the poet writing blank verse quietly and simply for his readers. Coleridge gave only one of his poems ('The Nightingale') the explicit subtitle 'A Conversation Poem', but he seems to have been using the word 'conversation' to mean something a good deal richer than it does today. The seventeenth and eighteenth centuries had used the word in the sense of 'living or having one's being in a particular place' and 'consorting or having dealings with others', as well as 'talk with acquaintances'. A 'Conversation Poem' would thus be a poem about how people relate to each other in a particular place, as well as how they behave and talk (to each other, to us).

'The Nightingale' is all about the shared experience of a group of friends. Coleridge listens to a nightingale and asks whether its song *is* melancholy or not (Milton says it is, but Coleridge suggests that 'in nature there is nothing melancholy' – *CPI* I. 517). He inquires whether it might be better called 'the merry Nightingale' (*CPI* I. 518) and whether, when talking with your friends, you might not even call its song 'wanton' (*CPI* I. 520) before, sadly, saying goodbye to them; they are the people you live among and want conversation (in every sense) with.

Even though you are saying goodbye, however, it will only be 'a short farewell' (*CPI* I. 518–20). In this ideal world of converse and conversation, such friends will meet again tomorrow. The poem ends with a memory of Coleridge's two-year-old son Hartley, distressed after a nightmare, being rushed outdoors by his father, catching sight of the moon and being transfixed by it: 'Suspends his sobs, and laughs most silently' (*CPI* I. 520). He is overcome by joy as is the poet; so ideally will the reader be, by the revelations of friendship, nature, nightingale and moon.

In 'This Lime Tree Bower my Prison', the narrator finds himself marooned with a bad foot, obliged to stay at home while his friends all go for a walk; he misses his conversation with them – again, in both the old and the modern senses – but imaginatively accompanies them and thus brings them all together.

It turns out that 'conversation' in its extended meaning goes to the heart of many of Coleridge's early poems; for example, 'The Eolian Harp', 'Reflections on Having Left a Place of Retirement' and 'Fears in Solitude'. All are concerned with the friendship and support which individuals, a particular place and a group can bring to the narrator, and in that way occupy an interestingly opposite ground to the exploration in the 'great poems' of power, terror and extreme states.

The only problem with identifying these two kinds of poetry is that they may distract attention from other poems which certainly should not be neglected. 'The Devil's Thoughts' (1799) and 'A Soliloquy of the Full Moon, She Being in a Mad Passion' (1802), for example, exploit Coleridge's love of the grotesque, the comic and the satirical, as well as demonstrating his facility as a versifier and rhymer. The first was written jointly with Southey, but many of the best stanzas are Coleridge's:

> He saw a lawyer killing a viper
> On the dunghill beside his stable;
>   Oh – oh; quoth he, for it put him in mind
>   Of the story of Cain and Abel.
>
>   . . .
> General – 's burning face
>   He saw with consternation,
> And back to Hell his way did take,
>   For the Devil thought, by a slight mistake,
>   It was General Conflagration.
>
>   (*CPI* i. 561, 566–7)

Coleridge is enjoying himself hugely as he scores points off his targets, political, social and religious. The 'Soliloquy' (first published in 1955) celebrates the way poets use the moon in their poetry, from the point of view of the contemptuous moon. The moon angrily describes how Wordsworth, 'head of the Gang', has turned him into 'a little canoe' (a recollection of the 'pointed horns of my canoe' described in Wordsworth's early poem 'Peter Bell'), before he goes on to settle scores with Coleridge:

> When one Coleridge, a Raff of the self-same Banditti
>   Past by – & intending no doubt to be witty,
> Because I'd the ill-fortune his taste to displease,
>   He turned up his nose,
>   And in pitiful Prose
> Made me into the half of a small Cheshire Cheese.
>
>   (*CPI* i. 692–3)

Coleridge's rhymes are spectacular and his high spirits contagious. The sixty-six-line poem was written within a fortnight of the first drafts of the 'Letter' poem. Coleridge's 'Dejection' was by no means the *only* emotion he was experiencing at the time; he was demonstrating, once again, his sheer range as a writer.

'Letter' poems and 'Dejection'

What was arguably the last major poem Coleridge wrote (major in the sense of its length, of the time he gave himself to write it and of its ambitions) was the poem now known variously as 'A Letter to –', 'A Letter to – April 4, 1802. – Sunday Evening' and 'Dejection: An Ode, written April 4, 1802', the last being a revised and shorter version of the poem, published in October 1802.

The real point of including 'Sunday Evening' in the title on the copy which Coleridge gave to the Wordsworths was to locate and memorialise the poem's inception at a particular moment; when the Wordsworths were staying a couple of nights with the Coleridges at their house Greta Hall, Keswick, in the Lake District, with William on his way on the morning of Monday 5 April to Sockburn, to see Mary (and Sara) Hutchinson, while Dorothy went part of the way with him but then stayed with friends at the head of Ullswater. On Saturday 3 April William had almost certainly read Coleridge what he had composed of his 'Immortality Ode', started the day before.

Coleridge's 'Letter' poem is in all kinds of ways a response to Wordsworth's poem: an imitation of it, a response to it, a carrying of it forward. The very first 'Letter' may even have been designed for Wordsworth, setting out to Sockburn, to take to Sara, and Wordsworth may have taken the first version of the poem with him. The poem suggests that its composition ran from sunset to midnight at least, but it certainly took longer; and with friends in the house on the 4th, too, it would have been most unlikely for Coleridge to have spent the whole of the evening in his study writing.

What had perhaps been originally envisaged as a few lines of verse grew into a poem of considerable length, because it came to be not just a letter to Sara but an analysis of what Coleridge thought was wrong with him, and how that linked with his feelings for Sara. On the one hand he found himself doing exactly what Wordsworth's 'Immortality' Ode had started to do. He insists that he has changed; that the things that at one time he could love and rejoice over are no longer there for him. 'I *see*, not *feel*, how beautiful they are!' (*CPI* II. 866). There is a good deal in the poem of this kind; the narrator insists how each 'Visitation' (as he calls it) of depression and dejection

'Suspends . . . My shaping Spirit of Imagination' (*CPII* 11. 871). This is one of the poem's centres.

Another is the letter to Sara, which is very concerned with the fact that although loving her, he has recently hurt her – has indeed made her ill. He now advises her to stay at home with those whose love she is sure of; he insists that he is no longer demanding to see her. All he needs to be certain of is that she is all right.

But he also writes a long section about a howling wind which reminds him of a child screaming for its lost mother. We can be reasonably sure of a subtext here; the narrator, agonised as he is, and unable to sleep as he thinks through his predicament, identifies with the child. The adult is lost in the same way as the child about whom Coleridge would write, years later: 'The witness of its own being had been suspended in the loss of the mother's presence' (*OM* 134). It *cannot* be itself without the endorsement of its mother.

He is also concerned with the child who grew up into an adult; an adult now married to the wrong person and condemned to depression. The poem at this point oscillates between its concern for Sara and its concern for its narrator. Coleridge sent Dorothy a letter a few days later – one she found immensely distressing – which suggests that it may well have contained yet another form of the 'Letter', one perhaps including some of the lines about his own unhappiness. In July the poem seems still to have been in progress.[18]

The poem indeed exists in many forms. It is a poem-letter to Sara as well as a poem-letter to Wordsworth; in a cut-down version, 'Dejection' is addressed to 'Edmund' and would be published as a kind of wedding present for Wordsworth and Mary Hutchinson in October. There is also a cut-down version addressed to 'a Lady', consisting of extensive selections in a letter to William Sotheby; there is also a good deal of the same poem in a letter to the Beaumonts in 1803. It may even once have been addressed to Tom Poole.

This suggests two things. Firstly, that perhaps there never *was* a 'final form' of the poem towards which Coleridge was working. He was writing poetry; perhaps he started that Sunday evening, but quite likely earlier (some 1801 notebook jottings get very close to the poem's text). And the poetry was added to, cut down, developed, over a period of time. Secondly, what he was writing about was not just his love for Sara, or his own failed marriage, or his friendship with Wordsworth, or even his sense of what had gone wrong in his own life, though all these things are in the poem. He was once again writing about a community of people, men and women, supporting and loving each other, the hope of which kept him sustained, the lack of which depressed him horribly. The 'Letter' poems were addressed to the group, brothers and sisters all; its members could read such poems in their own way. The poems were in fact the last of the 'conversation' poems, though fuelled by the imagination of rejection and loneliness.

'Asra' poems

Coleridge's love for Sara Hutchinson, from which the 'Letter' poems sprang, needed to be kept private and poems like the sonnet 'To Asra' were mostly unpublishable, the loving encoding being no real disguise. The original of another poem, 'The Blossoming of the Solitary Date Tree' (*CPI* ii. 811–13), which Coleridge never published, deploys some of the feelings, but the poem he revised and much later published utterly disguises their object. There were still other poems, some of them remaining concealed in his notebooks, like 'Recollections of Love', some eventually emerging disguised, such as 'All Look or Likeness' (*CPI* ii. 774–6).

They fascinate modern readers because of the biographical light they seem to throw on Coleridge's feelings for Sara. 'All Look or Likeness' is especially valuable in this respect because it consciously discounts (as 'accident') the physical appearance of the person addressed (Coleridge calls her 'the very Isulia', another of his special names for Sara/Asra), and paradoxically attempts to recreate the beloved person as an essential 'She, She alone, and only She', who manages to shine 'thro' her body visibly'. How, if an image is visible, can it have nothing to do with a body – unless it be a ghost of some kind? – but the point of the poem is its worship of the 'Image – all *her own!*' which suggests an identity a great deal more actual than phantasmal; Coleridge only added the title 'Phantom' many years after the poem had been written (*CPI* ii. 763).

It is a poem which might have been about the helpless idealisation of a beloved person; a subject Coleridge would, for example, brilliantly create in 'Constancy to an Ideal Object', with its final image of a man madly pursuing a phantasm, utterly unaware that it is he who '*makes* the shadow he pursues!' (*CPI* ii. 778). Not for nothing had Coleridge been fascinated with the phenomenon of the Brocken spectre while in the Harz mountains in 1799. One problem with 'All Look or Likeness' is that the poem seems, urgently and unironically, to be insisting on the very kind of 'Constancy to an Ideal Object' that the later poem shows to be 'but in the brain' (*CPI* ii. 777), not to say crazy if applied to a real person. Coleridge knew a lot about love and about his own capacity for idealisation; his fascination with both the real and the unreal revealed, indeed, how in his mind they 'may blend'.[19]

Theatre writing

It is natural to view Coleridge's theatre writing as part of his poetic output: his play *Osorio* of 1797 (heavily revised as *Remorse* in 1812–13) and in particular the translations he made between 1799 and 1800 of two *Wallenstein* plays by the German dramatist Friedrich Schiller. The latter are worth investigating as the outcomes of excitement with Schiller's work combining with a mind steeped in Shakespearean dramatic language, and illuminated at moments by a real poetic gift. Coleridge, however, professed himself desperately bored by the 'irksome & soul-wearying Labor' (*CL* I. 587) of translations that he had undertaken primarily for money ('*never, never, never* will I be so taken in again') and he was even ruder about *Osorio*: 'I would rather mend hedges and follow the plough, than write another' (*CL* I. 583, 356). Like the translations, *Osorio* contains a good deal of admirable poetry, unfortunately entombed in a terrible plot and articulated by characters whose author has no inkling how to make convincing. His outline sketch of the psychological realism he was aiming at in the character of Osorio – 'in truth a weak man yet always duping himself into the belief that he has a soul of Iron' (*CPIII* I. 150) – is far more convincing than the melodrama he actually wrote.

The 1812–13 version of the play is now chiefly intriguing because it demonstrates what successful, serious tragedy was like on the English stage at that date; it was important to Coleridge as a commercial and financial success, but one would not be surprised at being told that someone other than Coleridge (someone who knew their Shakespeare) had written it.

Later poetry

After 1802, Coleridge started and finished much less poetry. His own sense of failure as a poet is the reason usually adduced, and it is true that in September 1800 he declared, during his struggles to complete 'Christabel', that 'I abandon Poetry altogether', and he repeated the idea in December: 'I have altogether abandoned it . . . I mistook a strong desire for original power' (*CL* I. 623, 656). He obviously did not give it up, as poem after poem shows, but a number of reasons exist for his writing with less concentration. One was his conviction that Wordsworth was the poet, not he. Another was the fact that 'Christabel' had been such a struggle. There was also his growing belief that it was *his* life's work to write a major philosophical book about the basis of our experience, to which he believed he should be dedicating all his powers – and, compared with which, poetry seemed distinctly less important.

This was what he told Godwin in March 1801:

> all sounds of similitude keep at such distance from each other in my
> mind, that I have *forgotten* how to make a rhyme . . . I look at the
> Mountains only for the Curves of their outlines; the Stars, as I behold
> them, form themselves into Triangles – and my hands are scarred with
> scratches from a Cat, whose back I was rubbing in the Dark in order to
> see whether the sparks from it were refrangible by a Prism. The Poet is
> dead in me –   (*CL* ii. 714)

These were, of course, only ways of talking, not confessional truths, but they
concentrate on what he saw as his duties as a writer rather than on his pleasures.
In 1805 he went further when he spoke about his experience of the 'objects of
Nature' – he gave the example of 'yonder moon dim-glimmering thro' the dewy
window-pane' – as demanding from him, in response, 'a symbolical language
for something within me that already and forever exists' (*CN* ii. 2546). That
language would always correspond to (indeed exemplify) his experience of the
divine. It would, ideally, contribute to prose about religious experience, not to
poetry about nature; it was to plans for such writing about religious experience
that he believed he should devote himself. The poetry, if it came, would simply
be an adjunct.

For most of the time between 1803 and 1815, except in very special circumstances, he found it impossible to apply himself to work of any length, or
to work requiring the kind of sustained application which had led, for example, to 'The Ancient Mariner'. He had always liked the idea of the extempore
poem, produced and finished in a single sitting, with a date to commemorate
it, even if the actual writing had actually taken a good deal longer. The difference now was that while in the past his extempore poetry had been laboured
over for months and carefully crafted long after (and sometimes before) the
inscribed date, his later extempore poetry really *did* tend to be extempore.
Following his versions of the 'Letter' poem, his notebooks from 1803 onwards
accumulated single lines, stanzas, possible beginnings, potential endings, two
or four line fragments, which his editors have sometimes generously inter-
preted as 'a germinating poem' or 'an embryonic poem' (*CN* ii. 2806 n.,
3053 n.) but which may simply be the scraps they certainly look like. Though
he remained a poet, he now exercised his gifts mostly in brief lyrics and only
occasionally in a longer piece (for example 'The Pains of Sleep' in September
1803 or the 110-line poem to Wordsworth of January 1807) which – partly
because they were intensely autobiographical but also began as impromptu
and extempore writing – he was able to concentrate on sufficiently to write to a
finish.

It was not just modesty that made him refer to the lines of 'The Pains of Sleep' written in 1803 as 'doggrels' (*CL* II. 984) or decide not to publish them until 1816. Like the longer versions of the 'Letter' poems, they did not amount to a poem intended for publication; they were violently personal.

> A lurid light, a trampling throng,
> Sense of intolerable wrong,
> And whom I scorn'd, those only strong!

The fact that the versions he sent to Southey and Poole in 1803, the lines he sent to Henry Daniel in 1814 and the version he finally printed in 1816 (*CL* II. 982–4, II. 1009–10, III. 495–6, *CPI* I. 753–5) are all so different is a sign both of his astonishing facility and of the fact that it is not *these* words in *this* order[20] which make 'The Pains of Sleep' a poem. It is a series of excellent lines, couplets and triplets which could easily have consisted of (and at times actually employed) other excellent lines, couplets and triplets. Only in some of his continued revisions for 'The Ancient Mariner' – for example, the extra lines composed around October 1806 (*CN* II. 2880, *CPI* I. 389) – did he recapture the intense quality of any of the three great poems, and that perhaps only because the music of 'The Ancient Mariner' was something he had long internalised and could go on imitating and developing.

The idea that poetry might take a long time to write, so powerful an idea in Coleridge's early years – he remarked to Cottle in 1797 that 'I should not think of devoting less than 20 years to an Epic Poem' (*CL* I. 320) – was one that by 1803 he had pretty well abandoned. After the 'Letter' poems, he tended to go for immediate returns and generally failed to give his poetry-writing the concentration that he had once devoted to it. Even when he returned to his early 'Destiny of Nations' poem (partly constructed out of his contributions to Southey's poem *Joan of Arc*), his revision was neither consistent nor careful: 'The poem never received C's unremitting attention' (*CPI* I. 280).

Does it matter that his later poems and fragments are not as good as his early work? It would have done to Coleridge. He commented in 1804: 'If I do not like a poem, I can in my own conceit at least show a reason why *no* one ought to like [it]/or that they would be better off if they did not' (*CN* II. 2011). In the case of a poet with a large body of published poetry (there are 706 individual items in the most recent *Poetical Works*, the last 400 or so dating from after 1802), trying to give reasons why the later poetry is less good than the early is useful. My argument suggests that, after 1802, Coleridge grew sufficiently out of practice as a poet not to write poetry as seriously or as concentratedly as he had once done, although his gifts of language and for rhyming and rhythm continued to allow him adept solutions, especially in very short poems or in fragmentary writings. When he tried for something more weighty or complex, the writing tended to become stiff. Even so personal a poem as 'Work without Hope', from 1827, only goes through the motions (though Coleridge knows very well what those motions are). It does not address itself to his feelings:

> Yet well I ken the banks where amaranths blow,
> Have traced the fount whence streams of nectar flow.
> Bloom, O ye amaranths! bloom for whom ye may,
> For me ye bloom not! Glide, rich streams, away!
> With lips unbrightened, wreathless brow, I stroll:
> And would you learn the spells that drowse my soul?
> (*CPI* II. 1033)

At times it feels mannered and second-hand (e.g. the phrase 'I ken'). The last line comes as a shock; its language starts to *say* something, it does not simply deploy conventions. *OED* credits this poem with the first use of the odd word 'unbrightened', while 'drowse' as a transitive verb is seventeenth-century; towards the end of the poem, Coleridge *is* working harder, is stretching himself. Yet the complexity and effusiveness of his later prose-writing suggest that his habit of qualifying, and further qualifying, his thinking had grown inimical to the kinds of brevity, lucidity and point which poetry commonly demands.

A great deal of outstanding poetry-writing therefore appears in Coleridge's poetic oeuvre after 1802, but few good poems. I suggest that, rather than being holed below the waterline in 1800 by Wordsworth's attitude to 'Christabel', Coleridge – aware that he was not writing well, because he knew what he was capable of doing and had done – eventually came not to believe in himself as a poet. His best fully-fledged later poems were accomplished light verse, like the comic self-portrait in 'A Character' of 1819 and the slightly more serious 'Youth and Age' of 1823:

> Ah, woful WHEN!
> Ah for the change 'twixt Now and Then!
> This breathing House not built with hands,
> This body that does me grievous wrong,
> O'er aery Cliffs and glittering Sands,
> How lightly *then* it flashed along . . .
> Nought cared this Body for wind or weather
> When YOUTH and I liv'd in't together.
> (*CPI* II. 1012)

The effect of simple poignancy here was, for once, worked for; his notebooks contained draft after draft of the poem. Claims have been made for the merits of 'Alice du Clos or The Forked Tongue: A Ballad' on the grounds that it gathers together 'the tangled themes of jealousy that he experienced in 1806 . . . and 1810',[21] but it was written twenty years later and is no more than a fake gothic ballad (Coleridge even forgets his heroine's name at one point). Its main use today, perhaps, is to demonstrate why he was so right not to finish 'Christabel'. Of the wholly serious poetry after 1802, it is worth looking up 'The Blossoming of the Solitary Date Tree' in the form in which it has recently for the first time been published (*CPI* II. 808–11); it is a weird, fragmentary text full of memorable lines, which may date from 1802–4. The fragments 'Limbo' and 'Moles', drafted together in 1811, are striking, while the biographically touching 'To Asra', 'The Pang More Sharp than All', 'Work without Hope' and his final epitaph 'S.T.C' will always find readers.

Verse-writing for Coleridge after 1802, however, tended to be done 'in his spare time';[22] his later poems occasionally provided a nostalgic or wry glimpse back into the past, but they no longer played a necessary part in his writing life. When in 1819 he summed up the work he believed would survive him, he included 'some half-dozen of my poems' (*CL* IV. 925), which would not have allowed much space for poetry written after 1802. Nevertheless, when late in 1833 he finished his poem 'S.T.C.' he included the lines 'Beneath this Sod / A Poet lies – or that which once seem'd He'; he had drafted the poem twenty-six years earlier, when it had started 'Here lies a Poet –' (*CPI* II. 1145). It was as a poet, even if a failed one, that Coleridge continued all his life to think of himself.

Notebooks

Coleridge's notebooks – with their 7,000 individual entries, some pages-long, others tiny, brilliant aperçus – have been described as the 'unacknowledged prose masterpiece of the age'.[1] They have been edited in a series of massive volumes, with notes tracking down most of the quotations in which they abound. Here is a sample entry; the view from Coleridge's study window at Greta Hall on the morning of 21 October 1803.

> – A drisling Rain. Heavy masses of shapeless Vapour upon the mountains (O the perpetual Forms of Borrodale!) yet it is no unbroken Tale of dull Sadness – slanting Pillars travel across the Lake, at long Intervals – the vaporous mass whitens, in large Stains of Light . . . Little wool-packs of white bright vapour rest on different summits & declivities – the vale is narrowed by the mist & cloud – yet thro' the wall of mist you can see into a bason of sunny Light in Borrodale – the Birds are singing in the tender Rain, as if it were the Rain of April, & the decaying Foliage were Flowers & Blossoms. The pillar of Smoke from the Chimney rises up in the Mist, & is just distinguishable from it; & the Mountain Forms in the Gorge of Borrodale consubstantiate with the mist & cloud even as the pillared Smoke/a shade deeper, & a determinate Form.   (*CN* I. 1603)

There is a combination of simple observation ('slanting Pillars', 'large Stains of Light', 'a bason of sunny Light') with verbal and literary inventiveness ('Little wool-packs of white bright vapour'), while the theological term 'consubstantiate', meaning 'unite in one common substance', suggests the paradox of solidity and vapour in mountain and mist. There is also a subtle play of allusion. The pillar of cloud followed by the Children of Israel in the Book of Exodus is never far away; nor are Plato and his theory of forms – Coleridge linked 'sunny mist' with 'the luminous gloom of Plato' (*CN* I. 528, 1558). He is too, characteristically, in spite of the vast solidities of the mountains, writing not about a fixed landscape but about process and change; changing light, changing mist, changing shapes.

Above all, such writing invites us to see the world as Coleridge does; we look with his eyes and hear the sound of his voice. We become aware of the natural world as very few writers in the early nineteenth century make us. More than any passage in Wordsworth's writing, such an entry suggests how the Lake Poets trained themselves to observe the world: 'go & look and look', Coleridge instructed himself (*CN* II. 2101).

The entry is also valuable for demonstrating his linguistic verve. He devotes himself to it; he relishes the language and writes at full stretch. No one else might ever read it; it consists of 'words unsought-for and untrimmed because intended for your own eye exclusively' (*CN* IV. 5436). It nevertheless demands his absolute attention.

A second reason why the notebooks are important is very simple; they contain so much of Coleridge's best writing. He knew that one of his problems was 'bodily indolence', but if he conquered his habit of 'dozing & muddling away my Thoughts & Eyes' and got up from his sofa before forgetting his 'interesting Thoughts' (*CN* III. 3420, 3342), they had a chance of getting into his notebooks – where they are now preserved.

A final reason why Coleridge's notebooks are important is that in them he makes entries 'not as asserted truths but as processes of a mind working toward truth' (*CN* V. 6450). That is one of the joys of the literary form of the notebook. Coleridge hates the idea that entries in a notebook might be regarded as his 'fixed opinions'; they are 'Hints & first Thoughts', no more than 'the suggestions of the disquisition'. He headed an 1827 notebook: 'Volatilia / or / Day-book / for bird-liming / Small Thoughts / Impounding Stray Thoughts / and / holding for Trial doubtful Thoughts' (*CN* III. 3881, v. xlix-l). The notebooks provide some of the best examples of his belief in writing as process, in every sense. For that very reason, of course, the notebooks also resist categorisation; if this chapter feels fragmentary, the nature of the material is one reason.

Figure 2 Notebooks in the British Library before rebinding
(*CN* I, Illustration no. I, opposite p. xx).

Keeping notebooks

Coleridge started making entries in notebooks around the age of twenty-three;
he finished with a stack of seventy-two (eight appear above), some filled,
others partially empty. Larger notebooks (one of folio size) were confined to
his desk, but smaller ones could be tucked into a coat pocket, sometimes to be
rediscovered when the coat was taken up again for a journey. Although there

are sequences of entries in all the notebooks, a chronological order has to be constructed from internal evidence; Coleridge always had a number of books in use simultaneously.

It has been suggested that he tended to make entries in the notebooks when his writing in other forms was not going well; there are, for example, almost no entries contemporaneous with the writing of 'The Rime of the Ancyent Marinere' in 1797–8; there are very few from the time when he was writing his 'Letter' poems in 1802; and very few from the period in 1815 when he was writing *Biographia Literaria*. This may have been because at such times he was at work for so many hours a day that he would have had neither leisure nor energy to put much into his notebooks. Coleridge was nevertheless a born communicator, and his flow of perception and thought had to go somewhere; we are fortunate that so much of it ran into his notebooks.

A writer's life: nine kinds of notebook entry

(1) More than any of the other genres which he employed, Coleridge's notebooks demonstrate his work as a professional writer. They were, in the first place, a kind of warehouse to store materials for his own later use. Hence the extracts from rare books – from, for example, the philosopher-theologian Duns Scotus (*CN* I. 1369). Notebooks with such passages in them became part of Coleridge's library. In April 1801, he read the sixteenth-century Italian philosopher Giordano Bruno in Latin and copied out lengthy extracts, though he confessed to finding Bruno 'far too numeral, lineal, & pythagorean for my Comprehension . . . it is for others, at present, not for me'. He then, however, inserted the memorable admonitory sentence: 'till I understand a man's Ignorance, I presume myself ignorant of his understanding' (*CN* I. 928). Even Bruno turned out useful in the end; Coleridge would use the extracts when desperate for material to fill *The Friend* in 1809. In August 1801, he got Sara Hutchinson to copy out, from a book he had borrowed from Durham Cathedral Library, a long piece from the philosopher and theologian Thomas Aquinas; years later, he went back to the notebook and drew on it. He copied a number of pieces by the obscure seventeenth-century poet William Cartwright into Notebooks 9 and 21, probably early in 1804; he did the same with poems by the Italian seventeenth-century poet Barbara Strozzi in Notebook 17 in 1805. In 1815, he would still be extracting pieces out of his notebooks for *Biographia Literaria* and would for example publish the old admonition about ignorance and understanding, provoked by Bruno, at the start of chapter XII.[2]

(2) The notebooks were also the place where Coleridge listed literary projects (books and essays), in order to encourage himself to carry them through. There are countless examples of this. He noted down ideas for poems, essays and books, for example 'my Book of Logic' and 'my Book of Calumny'; he planned a book to be called *Extremes Meet* and went on making notes for it for years (e.g. *CN* I. 1153). There were notes and synopses for forms unknown or uncertain; there was a book to be called *Moral and Religious Musings & Mournings*; he planned an 'Essay on Criticism' in 1801, referring to it as 'my great Critical Work' in 1804; in 1803 there was even the first hint of *Biographia Literaria*, to be written only in 1815 (e.g. *CN* I. 1336). There was a poetical work to be called 'The Soother of Absence' while in October 1803 he planned 'a noble Poem of all my Youth nay *of all my Life*' (*CN* I. 1541, 1610). Late in 1803 and early in 1804, he developed the plan for a book which he felt thoroughly equipped to write: *Consolations and Comforts from the exercise & right application of the Reason, the Imagination, and the Moral Feelings*, for which he made many notes (e.g. *CN* II. 2011) but never wrote. Late in 1804 he collected examples which he could incorporate in his 'wild poem on strange things'; at times he inscribed detailed sketches, such as the outline of 'a most delightful poem' in 1808 which, again, he never managed to write (*CN* II. 2334, III. 3263). In May 1828 he set out a synopsis of his proposed *Philosophy of Epochs and Methods* (*CN* V. 5868): a huge project, the last manifestation of the great work which he hoped would justify his life as a writer – and never started.

(3) His notebooks also reveal Coleridge assembling and developing projects intended one day to turn into finished works. A lengthy biography of the German writer and philosopher Gotthold Ephraim Lessing, constructed from various sources in 1799, was obviously designed for publication; while Notebook 22 contains forty-nine different examples of metres, in various languages, the whole series assembled over a period of years (*CN* I. 377, II. 2224). His long travel entries, too, were often designed to be written up for publication, as we can judge from notes such as '(here insert the poem)' at the end of one of the travel entries he made as he walked through the Harz mountains in Germany in May 1799; or 'Lay stress on this' as he noticed the lack of sign posts on the road to Scotland in 1803 (*CN* I. 415, 1427). At times Coleridge reproached himself for merely 'planning compositions', for laying 'too many Eggs in the hot Sands of this Wilderness, the World!' (*CN* I. 1517, 1248) rather than devoting himself to getting them hatched. Fifteen months or so afterwards, he re-used the image almost verbatim in a letter to Thomas Poole (*CL* II. 1011); a case of a notebook supplying material for a letter.

(4) Lovers of his poetry will also find a good deal in the notebooks, some of it only otherwise available in the edition of his *Poetical Works* edited by J. C. C. Mays. There are, for example, lines from 1810 describing the body as the

> Eternal Shadow of the finite Soul/
> The Soul's self-symbol/it's image of itself,
> It's own yet not itself –
>
> (CN III. 3764, CPI II. 973)

And in 1820 he tried out some lines about music which may have been designed to exemplify one of his favourite sayings, 'extremes meet':

> Music
> Sweet discontent
> Of a Contentment overflowing,
> Jet of a Pleasure striving with it's fullness
>   a joy that strives with it's own fullness –
> or Sweet Overswell and mimic Discontent
> Of a too full Contentment.
>
> (CN IV. 4736, CPI II. 992)

(5) He also inscribed remarks from people whose views he intended to counter, either verbally or in print. He made entries just before going to see Godwin in order to argue with him, for example, but he inscribed too the offensive remark by Adam Smith that it is the 'Duty of a Poet to write like a Gentleman'; that could be the subject of a stinging rejoinder (*CN* I. 254, 775). In 1803, the poet Peter Bayley published a book of *Poems* containing plagiarism of and attacks on the Lake Poets; Coleridge wrote out extracts and noted various directions in which a response to Bayley might go (*CN* I. 1673). In January 1804 he inserted into a notebook lengthy extracts from a review in the *Annual Review* of 'A School of Poetry', again probably with a response in mind; in 1809 he copied out a long piece from Pinkerton's *Modern Geography*, probably meditating an attack on it in *The Friend* or in a lecture (*CN* III. 3524).

(6) At times he reminded himself of things that he might develop in newspaper articles or essays. He prepared his notebook for a research trip to Nottingham to acquire further information about an instance of false imprisonment, for example (*CN* I. 236–8). In 1807 he inscribed copious notes about a legal case in the West Country; in 1808 he wrote down stories told by Sara Hutchinson's brother Henry about his experiences at sea and in 1809 he prepared material for an attack on Sir Sidney Smith, an admiral he regarded as incompetent (*CN* II. 3195, III. 3369, 3582). While preparing *The Friend*, he noted numerous

ideas that might become articles (the attack on Sir Sidney was one of them); some of them began to turn into those articles within the confines of the notebooks (e.g. *CN* III. 3591–2). At other times Coleridge simply jotted down ideas about major subjects of morality, philosophy and religion, but also about more trivial topics. 'To analyse the pleasures received from Gates' he suggested to himself in 1803, and in 1805 he inscribed a memorandum: 'to collect facts for a comparison between a *wood* and a *coal*, fire, as to sights, sounds, & bodily feeling' (*CN* I. 1707, II. 2414).

(7) He also saw what he might do with a literary idea, and there and then started to work it out. He read a summary which the German writer Lessing gave of a Spanish play about the Earl of Essex and translated it, turning it into a synopsis for a drama of his own (*CN* I. 869–72). In 1803, he read a play by the seventeenth-century writer Sir John Suckling, summarised and quoted a few lines, but also rewrote some lines from it in an attempt to characterise his love for Sara Hutchinson (*CN* I. 1363–4). He wrote a long account of Southey in January 1804, and eleven years later used part of it in *Biographia Literaria*. He also needed somewhere to make plans and at times extensive notes for the lecture courses he gave between 1808 and 1819; he copied appropriate quotations into his notebooks, made suggestions for the direction in which lectures might go, and developed their arguments (e.g. *CN* III. 4494–5).

(8) The materials that bulk largest in Coleridge's notebooks from 1806 onwards, however, are religious analysis and speculation, on almost every subject of the Christian faith; the notebooks record years of thinking aloud. He argued with himself, talked himself into various understandings, and thus generated the kind of writing which found its way into *The Friend*, in its 1809 and its revised 1818 versions, and into the *Lay Sermons* of 1816. He engaged, too, in furious philosophical controversy and synthesis; in 1809, for example, he set himself the huge, unanswerable question 'What is the common principle of the Philosophical Systems of Des Cartes, (Lock?), Berkley, Hume, and Kant?' (*CN* III. 3605), and wrote pages of notes as the beginning of an answer. On the other hand, later in his life even matters of scientific interest tended to acquire a religious application; facts he recorded in 1823 about the iron content of plants and seeds, for example, turned into an 'Emblem of Original Sin' (*CN* IV. 4997).

(9) The notebooks also record his language-learning; there is a great deal of German in Notebooks 3 and 3½ and of Italian in Notebook K (*CN* I. 419, 353, II. 2133). Being Coleridge, however, he made a game even of his learning. He inscribed 'sterben – to die' but went on: 'decease, depart, depart this life, starve, breathe your last, expire, give up the ghost, kick up your heels, tip off, tip over the Perch' (*CN* I. 350).

The notebook as commonplace book

It is, however, often impossible to distinguish between material in the note-books that Coleridge noted down in order to do something with it in his writing, and material that was – itself – the writing he was doing. The note-books serve as a marvellous window into Coleridge's world, as he noted down things which caught his attention. Especially in the early notebooks, he was constantly surprised and pleased by what he came across. He observed the way that farmers in Yorkshire and other parts of the north kept asses with their horses and cows 'for luck!' (*CN* I. 580). As a practising psychologist, he observed with interest how, having intended to write Charles Lamb a note, being confident that he would not be seeing him, on unexpectedly finding his friend at home he still took 'pen & note paper' and started to write to him (*CN* II. 1875). On Malta, in 1805, he reckoned how much his fingernails grew in a year. He then worked out their combined growth in a year, added in the amount he reckoned his toenails grew, and came up with the total of three feet, seven inches 'yearly . . . of Nail' (*CN* II. 2522).

Coleridge always enjoyed writing down what people said to him. He described a meeting in July 1803, for example: 'an old man resting in the Shade in a hot noon. I accost him/sit beside him/talk to him/he to me/become interested' (*CN* I. 1415). He talked to everyone he met, whether in the Lake District in 1801 – 'She'll gang like a daisy' – or on H.M.S. *Speedwell* in 1804, when a sailor described for him 'A neat handed Fellow who could shave himself in a storm without drawing blood' (*CN* I. 861, II. 1999). Coleridge rejoiced in his fat fellow passenger Mrs Ireland wondering aloud 'I don't know what I shall say to the Apricot Tarts at Malta' (*CN* II. 2024); a ship's carpenter countered 'a plausible objection' with '"O Sir! I shall soon plug up that Shot-hole"'; a sailor in 1809, questioned about 'God's mercy, &c', remarked 'Ah but I an't so much afraid of him, it ar' t'other fellow –' (*CN* II. 2655, III. 3486). Occasionally Coleridge repeated anecdotes derived from local people; one of them, about an old lady north of Bampton apparently ignorant of Christ's crucifixion ('Hope they havn't kill'd the poor Gentleman . . . O well – we live up under the hill here – we do never hear a bit of news!' – *CN* I. 744) would be remembered by Hazlitt, who published it in 1818. A very specialised version of writing down what people said is to be found in Coleridge's notes of the speeches in the House of Commons, illegally scrawled-out in the gloom of the public gallery to enable him to write up the debates in the *Morning Post* (e.g. *CN* I. 651).

More than anything, however, Coleridge wanted to give *outness* to his experience – 'Language & all *symbols* give *outness* to Thoughts' (*CN* I. 1387).

He was struck by an idea when looking at an illustrated volume: 'In looking at Knorr's Shells felt the impulse of *doing* something – pleasures of gazing not sufficient – if I can *do* nothing else with the beauty, I can *show* it to somebody. Sympathy itself perhaps may have some connection with this impulse to embody Feeling in action' (*CN* I. 1356). Coleridge's notebooks are not only a warehouse of materials but also a writer's effort to find language for experience and thus to 'embody Feeling in action', and (in that way) to '*show* it'.

The notebooks are in fact at times creative sketchpads, demonstrating his range of language and reference. He made copious notes when attending Davy's chemistry lectures in London in the winter of 1801–2; in the middle of 1803 he paraphrased and summarised material about caterpillars, moths and butterflies; in December 1803 he included notes drawn from a book on natural history (*CN* I. 1098–9, 1378, 1738–53). He also noted down and developed what he had said 'in this morning's disquisition', when people would have come to hear him talk (*CN* III. 4456). On board *Speedwell* in 1804, he acquired 'large stores' of 'unwrought materials' from images of ships and sailing; he inscribed, for example, some pages of a manual of sailing directions for ships approaching Bamburgh Castle in Northumberland (*CN* II. 2086, 2022). It is doubtful whether, where or how he might ever have employed such language or such information; but it was striking, and he had just encountered it. On Malta he spun beautiful sentences around anecdotes taken from a natural history book; fishes preying on other fishes employ 'nets of such meshes, as permit many to escape . . . So two races are saved, the one by taking part, & the other by part not being taken' (*CN* II. 2329).

There are also lengthy accounts of scientific compounds and experiments; in 1802 about chemistry, a particular passion when he was young (he knew enough chemistry in 1803 to know that particles of the recently discovered 'oligist iron' would be ideal for sharpening a razor); he regularly made notes about optics and colours in 1809, while in 1812 he used acids of 'a combustible Basis' to demonstrate the problem of the exception proving the rule (*SWF* I. 140–1, *CN* III. 4171). Later in life, he returned over and over again to chemistry and was baffled by the concept of the atom: 'an atom is a pig with a buttered tail, the instant you catch it, you lose it' (*CN* IV. 4555–83, 4646). What he was actually doing was building up his own special cosmology as he attempted a massively comprehensive view of 'God, the World, and Man' which could bring 'all knowledges into harmony' (*CN* IV. 4645, *TT* I. 248). All natural substances fit together; oxygen, for example, stands for contraction and the east, hydrogen for dilation and the west; flint is vegetable, lime animal; 'powers, strata, chemistry, and life are all correlated' (*CN* IV. 4814 n.).

Dreams, fantasies, terrors

He was fascinated by his dreams, 'the intermediate of Life & Mind-fancy' as he called them (*CN* v. 5677); he included extraordinary accounts of people changing appearance.

> I dreamt of Dorothy, William & Mary – & that Dorothy was altered in every feature, a fat, thick-limbed & rather red-haired – in short, no resemblance to her at all – and I said, if I did not *know* you to be Dorothy, I never should *suppose* it/Why, says she – I have not a feature the same/& yet I was not surprized –   (*CN* i. 1250)

There is also a fantasy of how Sara Hutchinson (he was persuaded she *did* love him) would seek him out: 'at length you come to me/you are by my bed side, in some lonely Inn, where I lie deserted – there you have found me – there you are weeping over me! – Dear, dear, Woman!' (*CN* i. 1601). Later entries would imagine that she kissed him and had children by him; his entries hover between longing and fantasy (*CN* ii. 2036, iii. 4348, i. 1669).

He also felt forced to try and understand what had happened to his health. During his thirties, he found the effects of doses of laudanum fascinating and attempted to reproduce his experiences under its influence: 'overpowered with the Phænomena I arose, lit my candle, & wrote' (*CN* i. 1750). He noted down optical phenomena and scribbled a note to himself about 'the necessity of writing & indeed of all other m[otion] IN LARGE' when making such entries (*CN* i. 1751, 1750 and n.); he observed 'the Effort in writing – compare this writing with sober writing' (*CN* i. 1768). At times, laudanum contributed to the vividness of what he saw – 'What a beautiful Thing Urine is, in a Pot, brown yellow, transpicuous . . .' (*CN* i. 1766) – as well as altering the appearance of things; the very words on his notebook page appeared 'hairy, ragged – with a rough irregular *nap* upon them/this last is the real feeling – & yet something resembling words written on blotting paper' (*CN* ii. 2394). At other times, opium produced simple incoherence, as in an entry made in April 1805 in a 'firm enough hand' about its effects: 'drowsy slips, painful struggling drums, leap up from within, start, wake, chill/and all for the nothing. Tree, yon door. –' (*CN* ii. 2528).

On the other hand, some entries offer the most hopelessly despairing accounts of his mental anguish. In 1803, for example, 'Slanting Pillars of Light, like Ladders up to Heaven, their base always a field of vivid green Sunshine/ – This is Oct. 19. 1803. Wed. Morn. tomorrow my Birth Day, 31 years of age! – O me! my very heart dies! This *year* has been one painful Dream/I have done nothing! –' (*CN* i. 1577). In 1804, on Malta:

The Fish gasps on the glittering mud, the mud of this once full stream, now only moist enough to be glittering mud/the tide will flow back, time enough to lift me up with straws & withered sticks and bear me down into the ocean. O me! that being what I have been I should be what I am! – (*CN* ii. 2606)

He was also anguished for years by the hopelessness of his love for Sara and his jealousy of Wordsworth. In April 1811, for example, he wrote about Sara: 'tho' *false & cruel*, yet how can I cease to think her true & loving! – *O agony! –*' (*CN* iii. 4071).

His childhood had a lot to do with his later terrors and needs, he felt; he included autobiographical recollections, like sleeping out all night as a child at Ottery and being terrified by the bellowing of a calf (*CN* i. 1416). He recorded his illnesses and feelings in illness, and in 1807 wrote out the physical experiences constituting what we can understand as withdrawal symptoms (*CN* ii. 3078). He recorded the terrible constipation he had on board ship between Gibraltar and Malta, culminating in the 'day of Horror', 9 May 1804, when the Commodore's surgeon came aboard with 'Pipe and Syringe' and forcibly injected a salt water enema. Coleridge supplied full details: 'Anguish took away all disgust' (*CN* ii. 2085).

Travel writing and the natural world

His notebooks demonstrate how Coleridge was impelled not only to find language for experience but to create the feeling of feeling. It was how he located himself in the world, as observer and interlocutor. When walking in the Lakes in the early autumn of 1800, for example, he wrote: 'September 1 – the beards of Thistle & dandelions flying above the lonely mountains like life, & I saw them thro' the Trees skimming the lake like Swallows –' (*CN* i. 799). The phrase 'like life' is crucial; the human being perceives that something about him, even though 'traceless as life itself' (*CN* iv. 4766), feels like those flying seeds.

He also regularly felt compelled to find language for and to write down what he saw, to make it part of his own world. He described some brown linnets he had disturbed, and observed enviously how their 'easy natural' flight embodied 'four motions' at once, 'in one beautiful Whole, like a Machine –' (*CN* ii. 1851). He first viewed the Scale Force waterfall in November 1799: 'The first fall a thin broad white ribbon from a stupendous Height, uninterrupted tho' not unimpinged by, the perpendicular rock down which it falls . . .' (*CN* i. 540).

He did a good deal more after moving to the Lakes in 1800; he started not only to set down immediate impressions but also the sounds of what he heard, especially the noise of water. The river Greta, for example, 'has a loud voice, self-biographer of today's rains & thunder showers –'; he also imagined 'A River so translucent as not to be seen – and yet murmuring –' (*CN* I. 1660, 1124). In 1814 he became conscious of

> The ear-deceiving Imitation of a steady soaking Rain, while the Sky is in full uncurtainment of sprinkled Stars and milky Stream and dark blue Interspaces – the Rain had held up for two Hours or more – but so deep was the silence of the Night, that the *Drip* from the Leaves of the Garden Trees *copied* a steady Shower –   (*CN* III. 4220)

In 1822, he suddenly noted 'Insects garrulous mutes – incessantly noisy, and everlastingly *mute*' (*CN* IV. 4895); no matter how loud, they were without language. Late in life, he combined his anger that Wordsworth was talking uninterruptedly with a recollection of the English countryside: 'continuous never-intermitting deep murmuring in the throat, with ever and anon effort of sound as if to retain the Auditor struggling to get away, & corresponding to the *Splash* of a Brook whose continuous murmurs are varied by here and there a rocklet' (*CN* V. 5909). In the winter of 1803, at night, he was keenly aware of sounds both reassuring and ominous:

> The Greta sounds on, for ever. But I hear only the Ticking of my Watch, in the Pen-place of my Writing Desk, & the far lower note of the noise of the Fire – perpetual, yet seeming uncertain/it is the low voice of quiet change, of Destruction doing its work by little & little.   (*CN* I. 1635)

The most touching sound comes in an entry of 1800. Coleridge and Sarah feared that their newborn son Derwent, like his brother Berkeley, was destined for an early death: 'The Child hour after hour made a noise exactly like the Creeking of a door which is being shut very slowly to prevent its creeking' (*CN* I. 813).

It is also clear that many of these entries, especially the early ones, reveal Coleridge's need to record what he had heard and seen. In Scotland in 1803, he insisted to himself 'Never, never let me forget that small Herd boy, in his Tartan Plaid, dim-seen on the hilly field, & long heard ere seen, a melancholy *Voice*, calling to his Cattle!'; and then, a few days later, 'O never, never let me forget the beautiful birch stems, like silver tarnished' (*CN* I. 1471, 1495). In 1805, excited by the Maltese landscape, he determined 'to go with my Pocket-book, & minute its features' (*CN* II. 2449). If nature reminded him of what he felt he needed, it also constantly suggested what he lacked. 'There *is* a something, an essential something wanting in me. I feel it, I *know* it' (*CL* II. 1102), he insisted; 'Sometimes when I earnestly look at a beautiful Object or Landscape, it seems as if I were on the *brink* of a Fruition still denied' (*CN* III. 3767).

Accordingly he spent pages describing the places he was journeying through, on his various Lake District rambles, in Scotland, at sea, in Sicily; he had his notebook with him on the summit of Scafell and filled in a page there (*CN* I. 1217). Sometimes he had to remind himself to keep making notes: 'Let me not, in the intense *vividness of the Remembrance, forget to note* down the bridging Rock' (*CN* I. 1495). On board the *Speedwell*, going down the Channel in April 1804, his first job after breakfast was to 'Write or transcribe my Journal' and he observed 'what a beautiful object even a single wave is!' (*CN* II. 1993). A day or so later he described the paradox of 'the beautiful Surface of the Sea in this gentle Breeze! every form so transitory, so for the instant, & yet for that instant so substantial in all its sharp lines, steep surfaces, & hair-deep indentures, just as if it were cut glass, glass cut into ten thousand varieties' (*CN* II. 1999). On Malta, he was fascinated by lizards and spent a long time describing what he had never previously seen so clearly: 'firmness of its *stand-like* feet, where the *Life* of the *threddy* [i.e. 'thready', composed of fine fibres] Toes makes them both seem & be so firm, so solid' (*CN* II. 2144).

Late in life, he would declare that he had never worshipped nature: 'Nature is not God: she is the devil in a strait waistcoat' (*TT* I. 95 n.). But his early notebook entries are the evidence of the extent to which he had once genuflected before her, as when he referred to the mountains as 'that visible God Almighty that looks in at all my windows' (*CL* II. 714). One moonlit night on Malta, too, 'Unconsciously I stretched forth my arms so as to embrace the Sky, and in a trance I had worshipped God in the Moon' (*CN* II. 2453).

It is also striking how often the notebooks show him naming the world he encountered. He set down the names of people, rocks and mountains, hills and lakes, rivers and streams, villages and hamlets. Sometimes he did this from the maps he had been consulting (and redrawing in his notebooks); very often, however, the names were inscribed exactly as he heard them from local people (in December 1806, for example, 'Thringstone' in Leicestershire became 'Stringston'). Again, he strongly believed in naming: 'If I . . . call each thing by a name – describe it, as a trial of skill in words – it may bring back fragments of former Feeling – For we can live only by feeding abroad' (*CN* III. 3420). So he demanded that the world around him be named, not only seen and described or loved and recalled. That desire allowed him to continue to 'feed abroad'; 'every Hill & every River some sweet name . . . if first heard remembered as soon as heard' (*CN* II. 2045). He would list cats' names, ships' names and dogs' names (*CN* I. 1141, II. 2030, III. 3382).

The lack of practical usefulness of many of the entries was often true of his 'travel' notes; for example, the numerous examples made on his first tour of the Lake District accompanied by Wordsworth in November 1799. He was not going to write these up into a book or articles; he was with a man who knew the place far better than he ever would. Much of the travel writing in the early notebooks shows how very much Coleridge enjoyed, perhaps needed, the sound of his own voice, especially in a lonely place. For he often preferred to travel alone. He described a walk with Southey and Hazlitt in October 1803, for example, 'thro' Borrodale into Watendlath, & so home to a late dinner', but added: 'Of course it was to me a mere walk; for I must be alone, if either my Imagination or Heart are to be excited or enriched' (*CN* I. 1610). That was one reason (there were certainly others) why he would part from the Wordsworths a fortnight into a joint tour of Scotland they would make in 1803.

He often started a new notebook when setting out on a journey; he loved the sight that, for a moment, made the foreign homely or familiar. Arriving in Hamburg in 1798, he found the house gables weird 'with more than Chinese Grotesqueness – But the Sky & the Clouds, & the Moonlight thro' them is as if I were at Stowey. –' (*CN* I. 335). Deep in the Harz mountains in May 1799, he noted 'Here the country very much resembles that about Dulverton', while on a cool, grey, 'cloud-spotted' day in Sicily in 1805, he imagined how, 'had there been hedges instead of Stone-walls', he could have been in 'Somerset or S. Wales' (*CN* I. 411, II. 2682). He could also be at his most relaxed when travelling, as he noticed in Scotland in 1803:

> So having mounted a little & seen that there was not probably anything more to be noticed, I turned back – & now my mind being as it were leisurely and of[f] the stretch with what delight did I look at a floatage of Shadows on the water, made by the wavelets of the Stream, with what delight that most exquisite net at the bottom/sandy + pebbly river, all whose loops are wires of sunshine, gold finer than silk/   (*CN* I. 1489)

He might be relaxed but he was as aware of language as he was of the world around him. I discuss 'floatage' in chapter 5. 'Wavelet' is a very Coleridgian word; he seems to have been the first person to use it, while he also appears to have been the only person to take the idea of being *on* the stretch (i.e. tense) and to invert it, so as to be *off* the stretch. The term 'gold wire' is not original (it dates back to 1513 at least) but 'all whose loops are wires of sunshine' feels intensely modern.

He had an eye for the new, too; on 8 June 1819, on a coach journey from London to Essex, he noted 'Road velocipedous throughout – dry, hard, level and dustless' (*CN* IV. 4543). The velocipede (a wooden bicycle invented in 1818, propelled by the feet) was briefly the height of fashion, but 'velocipedous' was Coleridge's invention.

Coleridge revealed

The notebook entries, like so much of Coleridge's writing, are very often a kind of alternative *Biographical Sketches of My Literary Life and Opinions*, as he termed *Biographia Literaria*; they reveal his constant fascination with himself. He addressed himself seriously ('how dear do these thoughts cost you, Coleridge?' – *CN* II. 2064), admonishingly ('Coleridge! Coleridge! will you never learn to appropriate your conversation to your company?' – *CN* II. 2193) and as a stranger might ('Mr Colerid' – *CN* III. 4492). The entries can also be frightening. 'I write melancholy, always melancholy' (*CN* I. 1609), he confessed in October 1803. An entry records the end of his visit to Gallow Hill in March 1802 and perhaps the end of his hope that Sara might love him as he loved her. He inscribed what the Notebook editors call 'A *very* large clear entry':

> Gallow Hill, Thursday, March 11th, 1802
> S. T. Coleridge
> Sara
> SarHa   (*CN* I. 1150)

The repetition and the suggestion of laughter (if that is what it is) remain, however, a mystery.

The notebooks, however, also remind us of his joyful energy of thought; confronting things he does not like, embracing things he does. After 101 words copied from a travel book by the American William Bartram, in which snake birds 'delight to sit in little peaceable communities on the dry limbs of trees, hanging over the still waters, with their wings & tails expanded – I suppose to cool themselves, when at the same time they behold their images below –' he ended up with a bird swimming, head and neck up like a snake, invisible 'except sometimes the silvery tip of the Tail' (*CN* I. 222). He had added the very Coleridgian 'silvery' himself. He was plainly pleased with this bird; the fact that it sat contemplating itself in the mirror of the water would have endeared it to him (he was in the habit of 'fixing his prominent eyes upon himself... whenever there was a mirror in the room'[3]), and he would have liked the way it lived in 'little peaceable communities', Pantisocratically. He might have thought of using some of the details later (Bartram came in handy when he was writing 'Kubla Khan' and 'The Ancient Mariner'), but there is no escaping the sheer pleasure that impelled his inscription. Such an entry is characteristic in particular of the early notebooks, but he was still making occasional joyful entries late in his life, as in March 1830: 'Sky deep & clear milky blue – Stars powdering, not prominent but not yet bedimmed – only softlier silvered' (*CN* v. 6254).

Coleridge's capacity for pleasure is manifest too in his inclusion of part of a snarling scholarly exchange between Horace editors and reviewers; the pomposity of one Dr Parr was irresistible (*CN* I. 278). Probably while holed up in Grasmere on his very first visit in November 1799 (the weather was awful) he copied into his travel notebook the whole of a grotesque testimonial about worm-treatment, from an advert printed in a local paper (*CN* I. 517). There were also jocular poems; one he came across in Germany, while visiting Goslar, provided him with an opportunity to create a surprisingly accurate English rhyming version in his notebook, with his corrections showing just how he ended up with the text he did:

> Es ist zwar ein recht gutes Bier,
> Die Goslarische Gose –
> Doch wenn man glaubt sie sey im Bauch,
> So ist sie in die Hose.–

> This Goslars ~~Gose good and staunch~~ ale is strong & staunch,
> Yet ~~strangely one by~~ sure 'twas brew'd by Witches:
> For ~~scarce you launch it down~~ ere you think, 't has reach'd the Paunch
> Odd's fish! tis in your Breeches!   (*CN* I. 429)

In 1821 he would have fun with the less-than-grammatical utterances of Sir William Curtis, alderman of numerous London wards:

> Here lies Sir Will Curtis, our worthy Lord Mayor
> Who has left this here ward & is gone to that there.
>   (*CN* IV. 4837)

Spontaneous versification was an endearing part of Coleridge's life with his friends, and the notebooks allow us to enjoy it too.

He was, too, 'an inveterate planner' and – especially when young – listed tasks as minute as washing-up, when to put on the vegetables for dinner, and the time it might take to clear the table, as well as the household's lack of things he reckoned necessary: 'Mem – A Cheese Toaster' (*CN* I. 281 n., 284). (He may have been attempting to set his wife Sarah a good example.) He carefully planned the days to come on the *Speedwell* (*CN* II. 1993), not realising that he would feel so wretched with seasickness that he would do very little. In March 1810 he set out a schedule for working on *The Friend* Saturdays to Mondays, on his poems Tuesday to Thursday, and on journalism for the *Courier* on Fridays (*CN* III. 3748), even though in the event he accomplished none of these things. He regularly drew up lists of distances and possible routes when planning a journey; he compiled lists of journey expenses; in Germany he made extensive notes about prices (*CN* I. 738, 1205, 748, 338). This was perhaps because he was contemplating writing about the journey, but also because he naturally made lists, as when in February 1804 he noted what he might take to Malta: '3 wash Waistcoats/6 nankeen Pantaloons' (*CN* II. 1874).

What do the notebooks omit?

Although Coleridge sometimes dated his entries, the notebooks were not a diary. Sometimes he made entries at moments of great importance in his life, but often he did not. His original meeting with Sara Hutchinson in Sockburn in November 1799 went unrecorded, for example, although other entries (e.g. 'The long Entrancement of a True-love's Kiss' – *CN* I. 578) suggested exciting things happening. It would be three years before he would decide how crucial that first meeting had been, and would make up for the omission with some dates and entries about what had happened: the revealing sentences in Latin, of course – he was a married man (*CN* I. 1575). In Somerset, also in the autumn of 1799, he had recorded 'The aromatic smell of the Poplars in the fall of the Leaf' (*CN* I. 472); in Keswick in October 1803, when inserting his recollections of his November 1799 visit to Sockburn, he also copied out the entry about the 'Aromatic Smell of the Poplar, especially in the Fall of the Leaf'. In Syracuse on 5 November 1804, the smell and its associations came back to him: '. . . as I was passing up the green Lane with the garden on my left on my way to the Theatre, Nov – Monday, the aromatic Smell of the Poplars came upon me! What recollections, if I were worthy of indulging them' (*CN* II. 2245). Although refusing to indulge his feelings and deliberately omitting them, he could at least memorialise them in a notebook entry made five years after his original meeting with Sara, and on a Monday – the day he now particularly linked with his awareness of her in 1799 (*CN* I. 1575).

At other times, less important occasions did get precisely dated, as on the evening when he saw a wonderful moon above scudding clouds: 'the crescent

Moon hung, and partook not of the motion – her own hazy Light fill'd up the concave, as if it had been painted & the colors had run. – Dec. 19. 1800' (*CN* I. 875). But none of the dated entries is so tantalising as one made in December 1806, at a shattering moment. The entry starts:

The Epoch.
Saturday, 27th December, 1806 – Queen's Head, Stringston, ½ a mile
from Coleorton Church, 50 minutes after 10/   (*CN* II. 2975)

He was in a public house, where he had probably gone to acquire brandy to make opium digestible; the Wordsworths, with whom he was currently living, had been restricting his intake of alcohol and (therefore) of opium. A later reader, however, tore out the next three leaves, so that we shall never know exactly what the 'Epoch' was, though Coleridge returned to the memory of that Saturday morning (involving a fantasy of Sara's naked breast) on numerous occasions; he would still be writing about it in code in 1819 (*CN* II. 3148, III. 3328, IV. 4537). Still more memories of Sara Hutchinson, written in 1809, went missing when another leaf from the notebook was removed (*CN* III. 3708).

As with his Latin for events in November 1799, Coleridge regularly employed foreign languages and codes to inscribe dubious material. Touring the continent with Wordsworth and Dorothy in 1828, he furiously scribbled down in German his irritation with Wordsworth: 'never on man's earth have I known so hard, severe, incessant, at all points despotic, an egotism' (*CN* V. 5902). Only a Greek scholar could have recognised 'me gale o' mast on', inserted in December 1803, as an English transliteration of '$\mu\varepsilon\gamma\alpha\lambda\acute{o}\mu\alpha\sigma\tau o\nu$' [large-breasted], while his own number cipher allowed him to include the word 'ensheathment', meaning sexual penetration (*CN* I. 1718, II. 2398 and n.).

He was happy to describe and sketch the 'round fat backside of a hill' near the Clarksons' house (*CN* I. 555, 798), something he and William and John Wordsworth had been amused by when they first spotted it. When however he noticed a narrow road cut into the hill nearby, he used German and Greek to inscribe what it reminded him of (the 'weiblich $\tau\varepsilon\tau\rho\alpha\gamma\rho\alpha\mu\mu\alpha\tauo\nu$' ['female four-letter-word']). He might have *said* 'cunt' to the Wordsworth brothers but was sensitive to what in 1804 he would call 'a foul or impure word' (*CN* II. 2275). Nevertheless, he really wanted the observation in his notebook: 'I never saw so sweet an image!! –' (*CN* I. 555). He would later be amused by an Italian dictionary using 'little cunt' (*Connelino*) to inform its readers that it could not, on the grounds of propriety, include the word 'cunt' (*CN* II. 2658). He wished to distinguish love from lust, and developed a pun on 'longing' and 'elongation' ('the elongation of the esteemed towards the vagina') but inscribed it in Latin, as if he would rather not write such a thing down, although the succeeding double-entendre 'Would to Heaven . . . that (in another sense) I could *write it down*!' (*CN* IV. 4848) is in English.

He may have wanted to hide such things from potential readers of the notebooks (such as his wife Sarah) or from those (like Sara Hutchinson) whom we know handled the books. It seems, however, that he also disguised such things because to him they *were* shameful; fascinating but inappropriate. In such a spirit he would refer to 'The solid $\pi\varsigma$ [piss] of Serpents' (*CN* IV. 4580).

At various times some or all of the notebooks were in the hands of others. Charles Lamb inserted entries; Sara Hutchinson worked as an amanuensis for Coleridge, especially in 1801 and 1809; her brother George inscribed a title page for a copy of Wordsworth's *Prelude*; Southey's handwriting appears, as does that of Coleridge's Bristol backer Josiah Wade. At various times, too, he handed his notebook to someone to insert information (a list of fresco painters at Pisa, the time of an appointment in Cheapside) while the Coleridge children also scribbled in the books. Later readers also played their part. After Coleridge's death, many entries connected with his attitudes to his wife, to Sara Hutchinson and about his opium habit were removed with 'heavy black ink, scissors, or even acid eraser' (*CN* I. xviii). Notebooks got lost; some on the voyage back from Malta and Italy, one in London in 1808, others apparently after being numbered by his great-nephew Ernest Hartley Coleridge (their first editor).

Reading the notebooks

There are four ways for readers to experience the notebooks: one ideal but impractical; one which is the least good; one which is better; one which is best.

The ideal way might appear to be to have an original notebook in your hands. They were dispersed after Coleridge's death; many are in the British Library in London, others in Toronto. For modern readers, however, the originals are hard to cope with. They contain a scrawled mixture of English, Latin, Greek and German, as well as coded passages, diagrams and few probable sequences; entries run from the front and the back, at times overlapping, and some are practically illegible (see Figure 3). If ever you handle a notebook, your first reaction will be fascination and awe, but your second will be gratitude to editors who have managed to turn a packed and at times incomprehensible jumble into the clean texts of the published volumes. The only sensible way

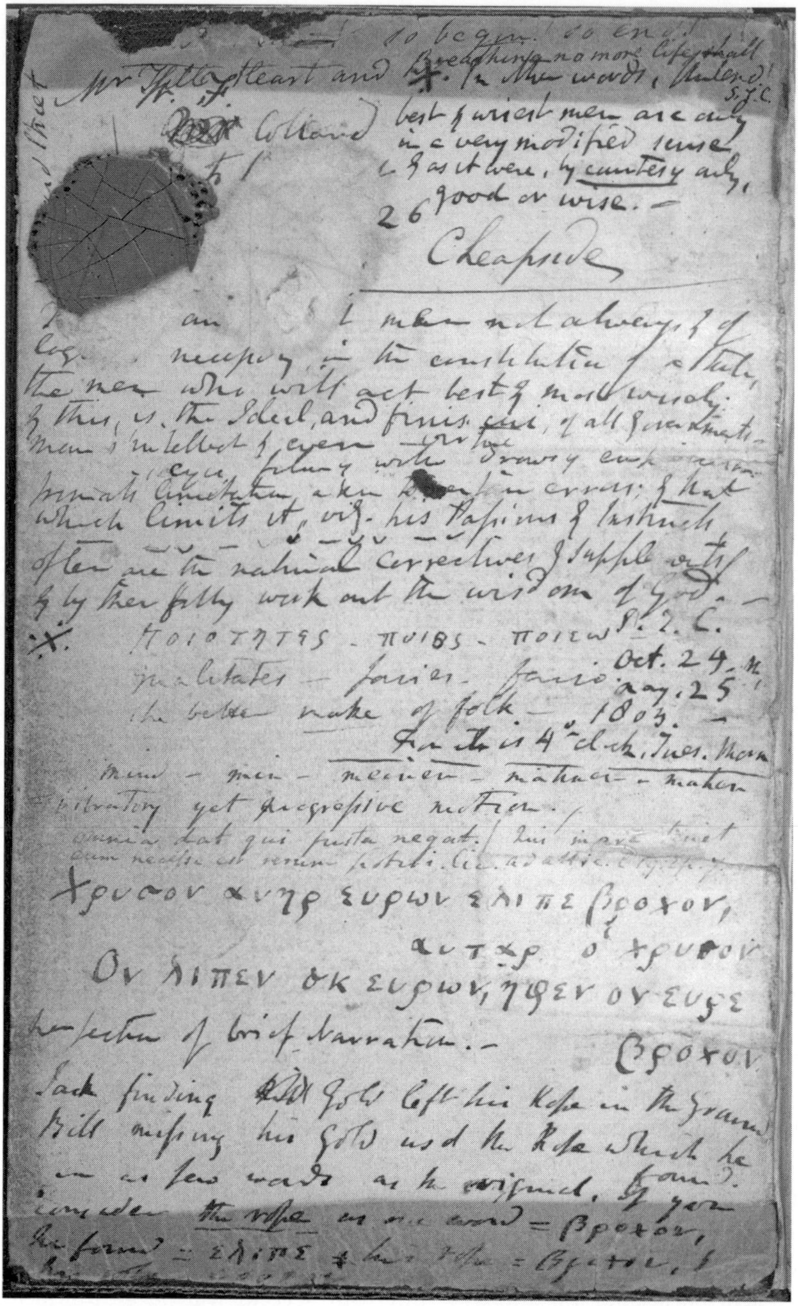

Figure 3 Inside front cover of Notebook 21 (British Library Add.
MS 47, 518 f.1ᵛ: *CN* I. 322, 378, 379, 1612, 1613; II. 2426).

to read the notebooks is in an edited or carefully transcribed version. (There should soon be web-based texts of individual notebooks available.)

The least good way is to consult the selection from the notebooks made by Ernest Hartley Coleridge in 1895 as *Anima Poetae* and still cheaply available. It includes wonderful sentences but it gives a misleading idea of what Coleridge was doing. Many of the short entries are plucked from the middle of longer ones, so that Coleridge often seems simply aphoristic, while the text is also unreliable.

There is, however, an excellent modern selection made by Seamus Perry which draws mostly upon the first three volumes of the Bollingen edition and will introduce any reader to a series of delights. What it will not, however, do is take you into the actual experience of immersion in the notebooks, when you feel bewildered, excited, irritated ('what *is* he going on about?'), illuminated, baffled, fascinated and constantly amazed.

The final way of reading the notebooks is therefore the only one I would recommend. You will need to acquire one of the volumes of the Bollingen edition text and the matching volume of notes, as well as the biggest dictionary you can manage (the *OED* in electronic form would be ideal). Lay the books on your table and start to read the text, constantly checking the notes and consulting the dictionary. Don't start with volume v, which contains a great deal of Bible analysis and is the least rewarding for the innocent reader. Start with volume I if possible; it is the most accessible and it also contains the whole of the so-called Gutch notebook, in some ways the most valuable of all Coleridge's notebooks.

But have a care. You will discover that, while reading his notebooks, you grow closer both to Coleridge as a man and to his main subjects of interest than when immersed in any other genre of his work. There are portraits as good as Dickens's: 'A Tall thin man stooping & bending in the middle tightly buttoned up, like a cracked Stick tight corded or ragged round the fracture' (*CN* I. 602). You will experience Coleridge's fantasy of the deep blue Mediterranean sea ('so very pure and one') being 'like a Night-sky . . . that turned round & lay in the day time under the paler Heaven'; you will imagine, along with him, that the world is 'not a total present, like a circle in space – but a manifest Spiral or infinite Helix in time & motion' (*CN* II. 2400, IV. 4989). You will be in danger of being converted for life to a belief that Coleridge's notebooks are one of the most exhilarating, if extraordinary, compilations of prose writing in the world.

Chapter 4

Mid-life works and contexts: 1803–1814

The years which might have been Coleridge's major creative period, from the age of thirty-one to forty-two, were seriously damaged by his opium habit. He wrote in 1805 about his 'sense of self-degradation' on consuming 'the long wretched Dose' (*CN* II. 2602); he brought his marriage to an end in 1806 but continued to suffer difficulties in settling to any project, crushing guilt over his failure as man, father and writer, and an awful sense of inadequacy. He suffered terrible bouts of pain; at times he thought he was dying.

These problems were succeeded around 1810 by his alienation from the closest of his early friends. He kept thinking, he kept reading (we find him planning to buy some £28 worth of scholarly books in 1808); he continued to write the occasional short poem between 1803 and 1815; on occasion he produced political journalism for the *Courier*, as in 1809–10 and 1811. But (with the exception of the enterprise of *The Friend* between 1809 and 1810) his intellectual and creative energies went into letter-writing, notebook-keeping, lecturing and planning books he could not write. At times, in desperation, he announced their readiness for the press, or even their being printed, when they were not even begun (e.g. *CL* III. 133; *Friend* II. 36–7). These years of 'despondent objectless Manhood' (*CN* III. 4048) were not only a terrible period but – apart from *The Friend* – in many ways a creative wasteland too.

Without any understanding of withdrawal symptoms, Coleridge continued to assume that countless different illnesses were damaging him. In February 1803 he had stated proudly that he had, for the previous four months, abstained 'from all wine, spirits, beer – and from all narcotics & exhilarants' (*CL* II. 919), but by 'narcotics' he would have meant drugs that caused sleepiness, not opiate painkillers. His confident announcement in August 1803 that he was suffering from the pains of '*atonic Gout*' may well have been made because opium was supposedly the best cure for it ('It is sometimes necessary to give it in very large doses . . . frequently repeated'[1]). As late as March 1804 he would announce that he had effectively dealt with a dreadful attack of diarrhoea by taking laudanum 'drop by drop' (*CL* ii. 1097). Things were still going terribly wrong. 'O Sorrow & Shame! I am not worthy to live – Two & thirty years. – & this last year above all others! – I have done nothing!' he had exclaimed in October 1804, while accusing himself of 'bedrugging the feelings'. His feeling of being an indolent failure agonised him; he grew possessed by an 'instinctive Sense of Self-insufficingness' (*CN* ii. 2237, iv. 4730).

In April 1804, he had gone to Malta, Sicily and Italy, in search of better health, and found himself engaged in the role of deputy public secretary to the governor. He came back in August 1806 without any improvement in his health. His opium and brandy habit had continued unchecked; an enciphered notebook entry of 27 December 1804 runs 'no night without its guilt of opium and spirit!' (*CN* ii. 2387 and n.). It was on Malta, too, that he experienced the 'melancholy, dreadful feeling' of finding himself middle-aged when he had previously always thought himself young: 'O Hope! O Hopelessness!' (*CN* iii. 3322). His journey to Malta took him away for a couple of years from most forms of writing (except for the official documents he worked on and his notebooks), while the months he spent in Italy between October 1805 and August 1806 were marked by catastrophic money problems, and long periods of misery and utter boredom. At times, the boiling of the kettle was the only genuinely compelling thing in his life:

> A Kettle is on a slow Fire/ & I turn from my Book, & loiter from going to my bed, in order to see whether it will boil/ – & on that my Hope hovers – on the Candle burning in the socket – or will this or that person come this evening . . . who when he comes neither gives me the least pleasure or does me the least good, as I well know, & have not the dimmest expectation that he will . . .   (*CN* ii. 2839)

One result was that he turned his formidable powers of analysis upon himself. He had developed what in 1808 he called a '*habit* of psychological analysis' (*CN* iii. 3355), and tried in his letters and notebooks to pin down and define the kinds of *lack* of feeling he had described in the 'Letter' poems ('A Grief without a pang, void, dark & drear' – *CPI* ii. 680). He had made a fascinating attempt on board the *Speedwell* in 1804, starting off with his longing for an absent person – probably Sara, possibly Wordsworth. As usual, it was in his notebook that he wrote, at a time when other kinds of writing, in particular completed or published writing, seemed nearly impossible.

> Why an't you here? This for ever/I have no rooted thorough thro'
> feeling – & never exist wholly present to any Sight, to any Sound, to any
> Emotion, to any series of Thoughts received or produced/always a feeling
> of yearning, that at times passes into Sickness of Heart.   (*CN* II. 2000)

What he saw, or heard, or felt, was never quite present to him. His emotions were not 'rooted thorough through'; they were not really feelings, only kinds of longing leading (eventually) to the experience of loss. In 1808 he would sum up such experience as 'I feel the anguish of not feeling' (*CN* III. 3353). He had had with him on the *Speedwell* the bulky manuscript of Wordsworth's poems which William, Mary and Sara had hastily prepared for him in March 1804; Mary had copied out the 'Immortality Ode' and Coleridge would have had a chance to read again lines such as 'The things which I have seen I see them now no more.'[2] But where Wordsworth's poem had constructed a philosophy of life out of his acceptance of such loss, Coleridge reacted more nakedly to his predicament.

It was, however, also the period when he moved decisively away from Unitarianism, and when he also started the process of rewriting his own political history, claiming in 1803, for example, that as early as 1796 'I was retiring from Politics, disgusted beyond measure by the manners & morals of the Democrats' (*CL* II. 999). His letters and notebooks from 1796 tell a different story, as does his journalism; as late as October 1802, he was defending the 'Jacobins' (to use the slang of the time) for wanting to found government 'on personal and natural rights' (*EHT* I. 370), while he remained close friends with Thelwall until at least 1800. In 1806, however, he penned into his notebook not just an attack on '*the People*' but on those radicals who styled themselves the 'Friends of the People', like Sir Francis Burdett, who advocated populist electoral reform: 'He alone is entitled to a share in the government of all, who has learnt to govern himself – there is but one possible ground of a Right to Freedom, viz. to understand & revere its Duties' (*CN* II. 2955).

It was a period of deep personal unhappiness; at times he was suicidal, especially during his last months in Italy in 1806; he had evinced a horribly self-castigating irony when exhorting himself 'look at the bright side always'.[3] He saw Sarah Coleridge briefly in the autumn of 1806, and persuaded her that they should live separately; Coleridge had hoped at least to be responsible for bringing up Hartley and Derwent, but the plan proved impracticable and by 1807 he had given it up. He thus suffered the effective loss of his children and the absolute loss of anything he might call a home.

From 1807 till 1808 he lodged at the London offices of the newspapers he wrote for. His first attempts at lecturing in London in the spring of 1808, undertaken to try and provide him with an income, were wrecked by illness (he had to cancel the lectures scheduled for February and March) though he then managed to keep them going until June when, again, he abandoned them because of ill health.

His continuing fantasy of love for Sara Hutchinson ('deepest yet hopeless Hope!' – *CN* II. 2517) did little to console him; it more often tormented him. This was true even when, in 1808, he returned to Grasmere and moved in with the Wordsworths, with whom Sara was also now living most of the time. They all found it very difficult. All were older, and more set in their ways, and Coleridge found himself reflecting, as ever, on process: 'only compare Dorothy with Dorothy of ten years ago – & just the same process has taken place with Mary and Sara'.[4] In particular, he was irritated by the admiration for Wordsworth evinced by the other (all female) members of the household. Nevertheless, Coleridge's project was – by regularising his way of life – to recover some of his status as an author by editing a new periodical, at first called *The Upholder*, but published as *The Friend*.

The Friend

Only in *The Friend* did Coleridge find a way of managing to write seriously during his middle years; indeed, he wrote almost all of it, over 140,000 words in all. It was not, however, at last a major work of major length. It was a collection (at times organised, at times random) of short and long pieces on subjects which interested him and its subtitle starts to suggest what a very odd work it was: 'A Literary, Moral and Political Weekly Paper, excluding Personal and Party Politics, and the Events of the Day. Conducted By S. T. Coleridge'. It was thus a political paper without politics, a newspaper without news, and neither written nor edited but conducted. It set out a compilation of philosophical insight, historical knowledge and reference, and lengthy discussions of abstruse subjects. The fourth number, for example, ended with a description of how God

> gave us Reason and with Reason Ideas of its own formation and underived from material Nature, self-consciousness, Principles, and above all, the Law of Conscience, which in the power of an holy and omnipotent Being *commands* us to attribute Reality – among the numerous Ideas   (*To be concluded in the next Number.*)

Subscribers had to wait a week to get the awkward rest of an awkward sentence:

mathematical or philosophical, which the Reason by the necessity of its own excellence, creates for itself – to those, (and those only) without which the Conscience would be baseless and contradictory; namely, to the ideas of Soul, the Free Will, Immortality, and God.

(*Friend* ɪɪ. 78–9)

It is, on second or third reading, lucid enough, but it *is* hard work; the sheer length, the parentheses, the absurdity of its being split over two issues. Subscribers were not given an easy time, though after issue 10 *The Friend* did at least start to include poetry and narrative too. But long stretches of *The Friend* are among the most unfriendly of Coleridge's major works, even in the revised version issued in 1818. He did not want to make it a popular or political paper; he aimed at quality.

Unlike the ten numbers of *The Watchman*, it was available by subscription only, and (with the help of almost everyone he knew) he had managed to acquire over 600 subscribers. And even though the paper would sell at a rather expensive 1/- for each number, it should theoretically have made him a profit of £150 in six months. The subscription system, however, was a disaster; no one paid anything until they had received twenty issues. Coleridge kept having to find money for the special stamped paper which a licensed newspaper had to use; and he had not done sufficient costing beforehand. Some subscribers who pulled out after twenty numbers (a number did) ended up paying nothing at all.

Coleridge kept *The Friend* going for twenty-eight numbers. It made him none of the income or reputation that he desired; he remarked gloomily afterwards that it had been 'printed rather than published, or so published that it had been well for the unfortunate author, if it had remained in manuscript' (*BL* ɪ. 175). Producing it probably cost him over £200 of his own money, and an astonishing amount of time and trouble (publishing a national newspaper in the Lake District was in itself remarkably difficult, and in Grasmere he was living some twenty-eight miles from his printer in Penrith). To help subsidise it, in December 1809 he wrote eight long Letters for the *Courier* in London about the Spanish Peninsular War, on which he was – as usual – well informed and superbly loquacious.

The Friend was one kind of response to the predicament of an individual writer of the period, in its attempt to create an intimate audience with which a writer might be in regular and personal contact (Coleridge's lecturing had been and would continue to be another such kind of contact). His problem was, in one way, very simple. The Wedgwood subsidy had to be used almost entirely to support his wife and children; and as a writer he could simply not support himself since he was mostly unable (literally, physically unable) to produce publishable work, except in the kinds of short burst which during these years enabled him to produce journalism and shorter essays to order, but not much else. And because *The Friend* was designed to be thoughtful, it was never witty in the ways that had made *The Watchman* fun as well as serious. Only at rare moments, such as the description in issue 8 of the ink-pot Luther is supposed to have thrown at the devil as an 'Author-like hand-grenado' (*Friend* ii. 115), does its tone lighten.

Oddly, it was when Coleridge was most desperate for copy that subscribers would generally have enjoyed themselves most. Some of the letters he had sent from Germany in 1798 (he had always hoped that his travel journals and letters might come in useful one day) made up almost the whole of issues 14 and 16 and a good deal of 18, while issue 13 consisted of a long and desperately sad story of two women in Germany which Coleridge insisted had been told him in person by the author and patriot Jonas Ludwig von Hess, the author of the 1800 book containing the story, but which Coleridge must simply have translated straight from the book, page after page, unacknowledged (the same was true of his lengthy account of Luther). In later issues, too, he included some poetry by Wordsworth, including extracts from the unpublished *Prelude*, and a number of biographical pieces about Sir Alexander Ball, who had just died.

Keeping *The Friend* going, as a periodical has to be kept going, was an heroic achievement, even if in practice it almost entirely depended upon the active involvement of Sara Hutchinson, who worked as Coleridge's amanuensis from the fourth issue onwards. Being able to dictate his text to her helped hugely; she not only wrote out almost every word of every issue, but also had some impact on regulating his opium consumption. The paper was nevertheless an act of financial folly; its payment methods idealistic, its finances never thought through. The fact that Sara decided, at the start of March 1810, to leave the Lakes and go and keep house for her brother in Radnorshire was probably her reaction to the demands Coleridge and *The Friend* were making on her. Her departure, however, may have brought Coleridge to realise that he too must pull out (he only managed two further numbers without her help). He abandoned *The Friend*, exhausted, before it bankrupted him.

Its failure was yet another proof of how, between 1803 and 1814, his literary career barely existed. He had no belief in himself as a writer able to influence the bulk of his contemporaries. The story of his servant girl making up the fire with unsold copies of *The Watchman* in 1796 felt horribly likely to be true about *The Friend* as well, with the quantities of undistributed copies he had left on his hands. He was, however, able to sell some of the issues, and sets could be made up by reprints which he commissioned (there was an 1812 edition, for example).

Those who had known him best, including the Wordsworths and Southey, had struggled on for years giving room in their houses and their hearts to someone who seemed certain, in the long run, to take advantage of their friendship and their kindness. Dorothy in particular became horribly impatient with Coleridge, having had him as a house guest for months during 1809 and 1810, and having tried to keep him off opium – and having (of course) failed:

> If he were not under our Roof, he would be just as much the slave of stimulants as ever; and his whole time and thoughts, (except when he is reading and he reads a great deal), are employed in deceiving himself, and seeking to deceive others . . . He lies in bed, always till after 12 o'clock, sometimes much later; and never walks out . . . Sometimes he does not speak a word, and when he does talk it is always very much and upon subjects as far aloof from himself or his friends as possible.
>
> (*LW* ii. 1. 399)

By now, deceiving his friends in order to procure alcohol and opium was habitual, and what Dorothy especially objected to; he knew he had 'an hundred times deceived, tricked, nay, actually & consciously LIED' (*CL* iii. 490). Dorothy also blamed Coleridge for taking advantage of Sara Hutchinson's willingness to help him; he had 'harrassed and agitated her mind continually, and we saw that he was doing her health perpetual injury' (*LW* ii. 1. 398). After Sara left the Wordsworth household, Coleridge wrote about her '*cruel neglect & contemptuous Silence*' (*CN* iii. 3912). He felt '*disrent*' (*CN* iii. 3796): torn in two. He even moved back into Greta Hall for a while, but there of all places could not escape reproaches for his indolence – which he hated; Sarah Coleridge observed how 'the slightest expression of regret never fails to excite resentment – Poor Man!'[5]

Relations with the Wordsworths had been awkward for months, but when Coleridge decided to go to London in the autumn of 1810, Wordsworth warned the people who were offering Coleridge a place to live just what a difficult house-guest he could be, while apparently also confessing that he had given up hope of his old friend ever changing. Coleridge discovered what Wordsworth had said and felt utterly betrayed, though he also seems to have seized on a reason for initiating a break. In June 1812, he would savagely enjoy adding bitter reflections to notebook entries made in 1803 during their joint trip to Scotland. In 1803, he had called Wordsworth 'My Friend'; in 1812 he added 'O me! what a word to give permanence to the mistake of a Life!' In 1803 he had planned to make his 'own way alone' to Edinburgh; in 1812, he added

'O Esteesee [i.e. 'S. T. C.']! that thou hadst from thy 22nd year indeed made *thy own* way & *alone!*' (*CN* i. 1471).

His life after *The Friend* staggered on into serious quarrels not only with the Wordsworths but with Southey, and members of his own family. In London at times he completely abandoned himself to opium; his friends' reactions varied from telling him to get a grip on himself, advising him to '*pray*', and asserting confidently that his cravings for opium had no 'bodily causes' but were simply the result of 'inclination and indulgence' (*CL* iii. 477–9). Southey grew especially savage, calling Coleridge 'the slave of the vilest and most degrading sensuality';[6] but it was Southey who had moved into Greta Hall with his wife Edith, and had taken on de facto responsibility for bringing up Coleridge's children in the absence of their father. Coleridge himself would always deny the charge of sensuality: 'My sole sensuality was *not* to be in pain!' (*CN* ii. 2368).

Coleridge and the operation of the senses

Yet, as always with Coleridge, it would be wrong to assume that these years were marked by uninterrupted failure and disaster. What (at times) *The Friend*, his letters and his notebooks allow one to do is to recognise just what a serious and resourceful thinker he continued to be. What his notebooks often present anecdotally, in the form of little stories of things that happen to him, are just as often serious reflections about the misinterpretations of our experience that the mind and body together conjure up. He gazed at Vesuvius in eruption, late in 1805, and noticed streaks of golden red fire down its sides – and wondered why on earth they started and stopped so arbitrarily . . . before realising that he was seeing, as lava flow, the fluttering pennants of ships in Naples harbour, far closer to him, which he would not have seen in that way had his mind not previously been filled with thoughts of the eruption. 'Logic Friend of Perception!' (*CN* ii. 2719) he noted, though he might just as well have responded 'Logic Friend of Deception!' On another occasion, in February 1807, he was walking at night in the woods near Coleorton with the Wordsworths, only to experience

> a sudden flash of Light darted down, as it were, upon the path close before me, with such rapid & indescribable effect, that my life seemed snatched away from me – not by terror, but by the whole attention being suddenly, & unexpectedly, seized hold of – if one would could conceive a violent Blow given by an unseen hand, yet without pain, or local sense of injury –

What had happened was that a large bird 'had suddenly flown upward, and by the spring of his feet or body had driven down the branch on which he was a-perch' (*CN* II. 2988).

The dislocation of experience in both cases – the difference between what the eye and the other senses registered, and what had actually happened – was for Coleridge profoundly significant. It confirmed to him what he had learned from Kant: the mind constructs experience out of sense impressions, as when he is so startled and believes that light has descended, when really a bird has flown up and a branch has moved. The senses not only convey the wrong message to the mind, but also grow preternaturally alert under the assault they suffer. It is hardly surprising that Coleridge had the idea in 1809 that someone should work through scientific publications collecting 'all the facts relative to the Senses, and to psychology' (*CN* III. 3587); he knew how well the two subjects went together.

A similar paralleling of experience had occurred during his reading of Kant in the late summer of 1809. His notebooks show him considering, very deeply, what sympathetic feeling is, might be and should be, according to Kant; but he then launches into an extensive, third-person account of the experiences of 'B' and his wife 'Mrs B' (versions of himself and Sarah Coleridge in the late summer of 1796). He describes the fellow-feeling expressed towards them (Sarah being pregnant at the time) by a woman whose child had recently died, and by her husband, who offered Coleridge a job as tutor. The theoretical investigation breaks off, the lengthy story is told, in considerable detail; then the theoretical investigation is resumed. Human beings are not only reacted upon by kindnesses, they are also caught up and actively involve themselves (if only via fellow-feeling) in the unpredictable actual events of the everyday.

It is impossible to write off such a writer as unproductive when he continues to report on his experience in such ways. There is some evidence of Coleridge making attempts, in the spring of 1809, to combat his opium habit with regulated and timed doses: '*12 at night only – no morn*' (*CN* III. 3484). But such details were only for himself. With others – even with the Wordsworths, with whom he was still living – he attempted to pretend he was no longer the victim of the habit or had at least cut back savagely. He had even promised Stuart's partner T. J. Street, whom he wanted to impress with his capacity for hard work and his renewed sense of responsibility, that he had stopped taking opium, having 'left it off *all at once*' (*CL* III. 125). Like any such pledge from a long-term user, it was quite untrue.

Incipient disaster

In London he attempted to get medical advice, but various things went wrong (he confided in one doctor, then quarrelled with him – and the doctor spread reports of Coleridge's opium habit). Between May and September 1811 he remained in London writing journalism for the *Courier*. He struggled through; in the winter he managed to set up and give a number of brief lecture courses in London (I discuss his lectures on Shakespeare in chapter 6). In 1812, however, another major blow fell. The annuity from the Wedgwoods which Coleridge had been receiving since 1798 was cut by half. Although Tom Wedgwood had died back in 1805, his £75 a year was still being paid; but Josiah had suffered serious financial losses because of the Napoleonic war and asked Coleridge if he could stop paying his own £75 a year. Coleridge had no option but to agree. Outwardly he was untroubled by the loss but, back in 1804, Dorothy Wordsworth had let slip how 'anxious . . . he always is about working and doing something when expenses stare him in the face' (*CL* ii. 1148). In 1812, his anxieties increased and increased, just when he knew himself less and less capable of 'doing something'.

He did have an unexpected success with a production of *Remorse* on the London stage early in 1813, from which he earned £400 (more than for all his other literary endeavours combined) though much of that must have gone in paying his debts. A good deal of 1813 is, however, almost a blank; we know nothing of what he was doing, thinking or writing. Letters between March and October do not survive, there is barely an entry in his notebooks.

By 1814 he was once again in a desperate state. He had felt suicidal at times, ever since Sara Hutchinson had left in 1810 – 'Well may I break this Pact, this League, of Blood/That ties me to myself – and break I shall' (*CN* iii. 3796) – while his laudanum and opium consumption were at a level which would easily have killed a person less habituated than himself. He reported to his old friend Joseph Cottle on 'the dreadful Hell of my mind & conscience & body' (*CL* iii. 478).

Medical assistance was his only chance; and for the remaining twenty years of his life it was only by giving up his freedom and putting himself in the hands of those prepared to care for him that he was able to function. He had first intended to take such a step in March 1808, but had been delayed by his London lecture course; in April 1814, feeling obliged to be deprived of access to razors and penknives, he again considered putting himself 'wholly in the Power of others' (*CL* iii. 479). It was not until he moved in for a year with the businessman John Morgan and family at Calne in Wiltshire, in December 1814, that he acquired some kind of stability, which meant some regulation of his opium use; but by 1815, he was in the situation of owing his creditors £300, and was prepared to engage in almost any literary activity to earn money.

Morgan was able to report in May 1816, however, that 'Col: goes on exceedingly well – he is reduced to 20 drops a dose' (*BL* ii. 287). Morgan had financial problems enough of his own, but was able to care for Coleridge and (like Sara Hutchinson in 1809–10) also took dictation from him, thus enabling him to use more productively his unquenched ability to think aloud. It was through being spoken aloud to an amanuensis that, with the exception of the entries in his notebooks, all the main works of Coleridge's later career, starting with *Biographia Literaria*, would come into being. On the one hand, dictation instilled in him an obligation to *produce*, which was not demanded of him by a blank sheet of paper in an empty room; but what seems to have been of equal importance to Coleridge was the contact between himself and the person taking down dictation from him. It returned him to the role of the boy talking impressively to adults, as well as giving him the status of sage: one whose very words impressed his admiring auditors. It is worth briefly examining the language of this man who, of all authors in English, believed himself one of the most 'wordly-minded' ('a most philosophical word' – *CN* i. 1725).

Language

Working hard to choose the right word was something which Coleridge not only very much enjoyed doing, but also believed in. 'We think *in* words, and reason *by* words' (*EHT* I. 114), he had argued in 1800. When he asked himself in 1810 'How the human Soul *is* affected', he had answered 'by Language' (*CN* III. 3810). In 1828 he first mentioned his plan for a book 'on the Power and Use of Words' ('Logic in it's living uses') which he was still considering in 1833 (*CL* VI. 967) but, sadly, never wrote. Language was not simply a consequence of the human being's receptiveness to sense impressions and reflecting upon them, as had been argued by, for example, Horne Tooke, the pre-eminent English linguist of Coleridge's day. Language was, Coleridge insisted, a consequence of the mind's capacity for conscious thought. 'Language is the medium of all Thoughts to *ourselves* of all Feelings to others, & partly to ourselves' (*CN* III. 4237). Accordingly, *thinking* played a crucial part in the human development of language. Words were not simply the 'mere names of things'; they *were* things, 'the great mighty instruments by which thoughts are excited' (*LPhil* I. 257). Language is a complex, historical structure which works in correspondence with 'the operations of the mind and heart' (*TT* I. 130–1).

The right word

In a lecture in November 1811, Coleridge offered a comic account of one of his own attempts to choose the right word. In August 1803, accompanied by William and Dorothy Wordsworth, he had visited the waterfalls on the River Clyde, and afterwards tried to find the right word to sum up his reaction. John Payne Collier, in the audience in 1811, made shorthand notes recording how Coleridge, after 'much deliberation', had 'pitched upon Majestic' but while still considering the matter had encountered 'a gentleman & lady'; and the first thing the man had said was

> 'It is very majestic.' – Coleridge was much pleased to find a concurrent opinion & complimented the person on the choice of his term in warm language. 'Yes Sir' replies the gentleman, 'I say it is very majestic, it is sublime, & it is beautiful and it is grand & picturesque' – 'Aye' added the lady, 'it is the prettiest thing I ever saw.'

Coleridge, whose own struggle to find the right word had been so acute, described himself as being 'not a little disconcerted'[1] by the abundance of wrong words thus washing over him.

He had been denouncing imprecise language since his 'Jacobin' years; the word 'legitimate', for example, used by defenders of the status quo, was 'so vague' that it 'signifies nothing but the passion of the man who uses it' (*EHT* i. 136). He had set out in the lecture which included the Clyde anecdote to attack 'The vague use of Terms' (*LL* i. 187), just as in 1825 he would state that the principal aim of his book *Aids to Reflection* was 'To direct the Reader's attention to the value of the Science of Words, their use and abuse . . . and the incalculable advantages attached to the habit of using them appropriately, and with a distinct knowledge of their primary, derivative, and metaphorical senses' (*AR* 6–7). Even though that was a book about religion, because words are 'living powers' (*AR* 10) religion itself is corrupted if its language is distorted or abused.

In his own 1803 notebook entries about the waterfalls on the Clyde, not once had Coleridge used the word 'majestic', though Dorothy Wordsworth remembered him using it.[2] The point of the anecdote, however, was to remind his listeners that 'majestic' is *not* a synonym of 'sublime', or 'beautiful', or 'grand' or 'picturesque' (or 'pretty'). Each word has its own 'primary, derivative, and metaphorical sense' to be respected. In 1824 he gave himself some good advice: 'Maxim. Never content yourself with the general meaning of a word, or with the equivalent senses too frequently given in the Lexicons as *the meanings*' (*CN* iv. 5136). He was a great enemy of synonyms ('defects in language'), but not just because they so often led to lazy, unthinking speech and writing. They were a kind of blurring of what was really in mind: 'one word in reality has but one meaning, tho' that meaning... may have 50 applications' (*CN* iii. 3780). He was deeply interested in how language developed: 'all Languages perfect themselves by a gradual process of desynonymizing words originally equivalent, as Propriety, Property' (*CN* iii. 4397). 'Desynonymize' was his own invented word; he would describe how 'a certain collective, unconscious good sense' worked 'progressively' to encourage such a process (*BL* i. 82).

Coleridge's fascination was with the multiplicity of shades of meaning in English, as well as his insistence on distinctions between (for example) 'reason' and 'understanding', 'thought' and 'attention', 'fame' and 'reputation', 'imitation' and 'copy' (*CN* iv. 4617, iii. 3670, 3671, ii. 2211, 2274). Together with his famous distinction between 'fancy' and 'imagination' (see chapter 6), these demonstrate the insistent carefulness which not only characterised his daily life but lay at the heart of his thinking, whether about poetry, society, philosophy, religion or science. Thinking of gold, he complained that 'Malleable as differenced from ductile is an ill-chosen ... sort of a word. Surely, expansible, or dilative are better. –' (*CN* iv. 4563). He would draw a simple, beautiful distinction about 'solid': 'Fluid not || [opposite to] solid but to rigid – . Solid || Hollow' (*CN* iii. 3572).

The language of thought

Such to-ing and fro-ing in language is an example of what he once described (when justifying his own use of parentheses) as the '*drama* of Reason'; he wanted to 'present the thought growing' (*CL* iii. 282). On the other hand, he was also aware that the same words can have 'many applications, and occur under different or even opposite circumstances. Board her! cries Jack Tar, speaking of an enemy's Ship. Board her, my Lad! cries Jack Tar to his bashful shipmate, speaking of the Latter's Sweetheart –' (*CN* iv. 5136). On the *Speedwell* in 1804, Coleridge took himself to task for misunderstanding the word 'shrouds', a word he must have been hearing daily for almost a month: 'N.B. Shrouds are the tight parts of the Rigging... This in memorial of my ignorance, who had identified them with the Sails' (*CN* ii. 2070). His assumption may well have been fed by the conception of 'shroud' as winding sheet, cover or tent, all commonly canvas; the standard 'Land-Lubbers' (*CN* iii. 3486) meaning. And because he knew that meaning so well, and it was roughly applicable to where the seamen were working, up the mast, his mind had not considered the second most common meaning, of ropes in pairs.

At times his frustration with *not* being able to find the right word showed itself: 'O Christ, it maddens me that I am not a painter, or that Painters are not I!' (*CN* I. 1495). While on the one hand he could write a rapturous notebook entry –

> The soil that fell from the Hawk poised at the extreme boundary of Sight thro' a column of sunshine – a falling star, a gem, the fixation, & chrystal, of substantial Light, again dissolving & elongating like a liquid Drop . . .

– yet he also knew how such language teetered on the edge of absurdity. Someone less sympathetic might simply exclaim 'Hawk's *Turd!*' (*CN* III. 3401). And though he would have liked to call such crudity 'blasphemy', and insist on 'divinely languageless' experience (*CN* III. 3401), he could not, as an adult, bring himself to attempt any such thing; language remained a necessary struggle. As he once remarked: 'Words not interpreters, but fellow-combatants' (*CN* II. 2356). Making a notebook entry about the mountains up towards Fort William, he began to describe how the ridge was segmented 'miserably' but immediately crossed the word out and inscribed 'variously', together with the injunction 'Silly words I am vexed with you'. Within a line, however, he found himself developing a new language for what he was observing: 'A File of Sheep among Heath, perfect Ribboning – It is an *intuition*' (*CN* I. 1490). No one had previously used 'ribbon' in such a way; 'to ribbon' had previously meant only 'To adorn with ribbon or ribbons', although fifty years after Coleridge it was being used to mean 'mark or stripe in a way resembling ribbons' (*OED*). The way in which a road or a long line of something can be described as 'ribboning' or 'ribboned' is (except for this single instance from Coleridge) distinctively twentieth century. When noting 'It is an *intuition*', he was probably thinking of how the sheep followed each other intuitively, but he might just as well have been describing how, intuitively, he had found an appropriate analogy and had stopped being vexed by language.

As so often with Coleridge, it is the process of thinking which really interests him; he is primarily concerned with the way that experience, language and the human mind act and react on each other. He knows that this process should be configured or described as a kind of interaction: 'Every new term expressing a fact, or a difference, not precisely and adequately expressed by any other word in the same language, is a new organ of thought for the mind that has learned it' (*C&S* 167). As early as 1798 he had condemned the obscenity of using words while remaining detached from their implications. The newspaper war reporter, for example, 'Becomes a fluent phraseman, absolute / And technical in victories and defeats, / And all our dainty terms for fratricide':

> And what if all-avenging Providence,
> Strong and retributive, should make us know
> The meaning of our words, force us to feel
> The desolation and the agony
> Of our fierce doings? (*CPI* i. 473)

Even the word 'idea' was too vague for Coleridge; in 1808 he would refer to 'that abominable word, Idea/how have I been struggling to get rid of it, & to find some exact word for each exact meaning' (*CN* iii. 3268). When he defined the poet as someone who is 'both Harp and Breeze' (he was employing his old image of the Eolian harp, hung up in a window for the passing breeze to play upon), it was with the same sense of the poet's mind being both active and passive, creative and responsive.[3] At times he feared that his writing had sounded simply 'like a play of Words', as when he struggled to describe the colours and movements of the sea; words being used for their own sakes, not for what they conveyed.

For Coleridge, though, it was never a matter just of words. The metaphors he employed were constant revelations of the ways in which thinking – and therefore language – operate. In 1795, he had remarked that 'It seems characteristic of true eloquence, to reason *in* metaphors; of declamation, to argue *by* metaphors' (*Watchman* 31). In his writing he aimed to respond to the local and also to create something of the larger effect, just as he had wanted to link the facts of the individual life to ways of understanding the human phenomenon. In this double form of responsiveness, 'the mind within me was struggling to express the marvellous distinctness & unconfounded personality of each of the million millions of forms, & yet their undivided unity in which they subsisted' (*CN* ii. 2344). That could be the urgent struggle to express of a man looking through a microscope or consulting a dictionary of synonyms, or indeed of a man considering his own society and its inter-relationships.

The origins of language

In 1817, recalling his early struggles as a poet, Coleridge described his attempts to identify 'natural language' as something which was 'neither bookish, nor vulgar' (*BL* i. 22). It should be 'the unpremeditated and evidently habitual *arrangement*' (*Friend* i. 449) of words. Like many of his contemporaries, he subscribed to the belief that the origins of language could be traced back to primitive sounds: the first noises made, for example, by children. 'B and M both labials/hence Infants first utter a, Ba, pa, ma, milk –' (*CN* i. 4).

His notebooks and letters grew rich in observations of children because Coleridge consciously watched them to see how they acquired and developed language and grammar. At the start, 'gna' was all they might articulate, 'yet we are not offended' (*CN* iii. 4349); it was a sound 'in which it is not difficult to discover the germ of the simple Negative' (*CN* iv. 4765). He speculated about a research project 'To trace the if not absolute birth yet the growth & endurance of Language from the Mother talking to the Child at her Breast', and observed that infants 'attempt to imitate sights & modes of *Touch* by sound, using the organs of speech as embryo hands, moulding the voice or sound' (*CN* ii. 2352, iv. 4726). He saw how 'Children in making new Words always do it analogously – explain this –' (*CN* i. 867). His own son Derwent, for example, at the age of eighteen months, 'extends the idea of Door so far that he not only calls the Lids of Boxes Doors, but even the Covers of Books' (*CN* i. 1192). Hartley came late to language; 'It seems to elucidate the Theory of Language' that, when he was 'just able to speak a few words', his father observed the boy 'making a fire-place of stones, with stones for fire. – four stones – fire-place – two stones – fire – /arbitrary symbols in Imagination' (*CN* i. 918) Coleridge may have been considering whether Hartley was responding innately to the need for a complex (or four-stone) word for the complex double-word 'fire-place', compared with the primary substance, which only merited two stones. By the time he was five, Hartley's linguistic sophistication was pronounced; on being asked whether a little girl with whom he went to school was 'an Acquaintance of his', he 'replied very fervently, pressing his right hand on his heart – No! She is an *In*quaintance' (*CL* v. 466).

Derwent (family name 'Stumpy Canary') was never so complicated:

> Derwent when he had scarce a score of words in his whole Tonguedom comes holding up a pair of filthy Pawlets, & lisps – Here's *clean white* Hands! – & then laughed immoderately   (*CN* i. 1645)

As well as paying loving attention to the child, and how he or she begins to realise not just the fun of lying but what linguistic play might be, Coleridge does so with words like 'tonguedom' and 'pawlet', playful coinages, neither subsequently accepted into English but appropriately primitive for the language of (and applied to) children. He was always happy inventing diminutives: 'cloudlet' (*CN* i. 1616), 'dastardling' (*CPIII* i. 503), 'goddessling' and 'godkin' (*CL* ii. 865), 'punlet' (*CM* iii. 193), 'Swimlet' (*CN* iv. 5025), 'toadlet' (*BL* ii. 178) and 'wombling' (*CN* iii. 3567) are all his – some accepted into *OED*, most not.

Late in life, Coleridge would develop an analogy for what he believed was the child's implicit acceptance, in a pre-linguistic state, of God's existence. He argued that an awareness of God is grounded, for the child, in its relationship with the world outside it, so that it becomes conscious of God not as a collection of individual characteristics (like the individual letters 'G' and 'O' and 'D'), but as a 'One & indivisible something': 'for the infant the mother contains his own self, and the whole problem of existence as a whole; and the word "GOD" is the first and one solution of the problem. Ask you, what is its meaning for the child? Even this: "the something, to which my [mother] looks up, and which is more than my mother"' (*OM* 131). When Hartley was six, his writing caught his father's attention; Coleridge noted 'Hartley's love to Papa – scrawls pothooks [i.e. hooked strokes made in learning to write], & reads what he *meant* by them' (*CN* I. 330). The child does exactly what the adult does with language; he reads what he *means* to write, not what he actually imposes on the page before him.

Grammar

Coleridge's thinking about language led him to 'his favourite topic, grammar'.[4] On the one hand, he wanted to believe in the coincidence of grammar and logic: 'Know essentially a verb active. If we know, there must be somewhat known by us. KNOWLEDGE WITHOUT A CORRESPONDENT Reality is NO KNOWLEDGE' (*CN* III. 4265). James McKusick attempts to sum up Coleridge's understanding of the forms of grammar as 'nothing other than the modes of relation perceived by the understanding and enumerated in formal logic'.[5] Coleridge, however, demonstrates an equal fascination with grammar and psychology; he insists that grammar 'presupposes a knowledge of psychology, or the laws by which we think and feel' (*SWF* I. 160). It is not formally or logically imposed upon human needs, but responds to them. He starts a typical notebook entry with the widespread but at that date thoroughly incorrect usage 'It is me', and comments cogently:

> I doubt, whether this be necessarily bad grammar, psychologically analysed. Who was it, did that? It was I. Who were there? I and Thomas and William. And which of you was it they beat so? – O sir it was *me*. – Here comes the true Objective Case.   (*CN* II. 2642)

His use of context and psychology, rather than precedent or rule, to assist in making grammatical choices is especially unusual, just as he writes at length arguing for the use of commas, full-stops, colons and semicolons not as 'symbols of Logic' but as 'dramatic directions'. Punctuation, he insists, 'is always prospective', 'not made according to the actual weight & difference or equality of the logical connections, but to the view which the Speaker is supposed to have at the moment, in which he speaks the particular sentence' (*CN* III. 3504).

Punctuation collaborates, that is, with the creation of meaning in a sentence, and Coleridge is especially concerned where grammar does not help create such meaning. He describes how Greek confuses 'under the genitive... the possessive, the instrumental or prepositional' (*CN* III. 3778); he also complains about the lack in English of 'a common gender in the pronoun adjective, his, her, and it – to agree with the word person, $\alpha\nu\theta\rho\omega\pi\sigma\varsigma$, mensch, and all words implying man or woman indifferently – such as Worshipper, Friend, &c &c' (*CN* III. 3399).

Words as things

Coleridge's linguistic sophistication did not, however, lead him into much accuracy about the derivations he propounded. His etymologies, following those of Horne Tooke (both men were working before the development of modern philology), were at best speculative and at times fantastic.

In 1799, Coleridge would set down the sequence 'Till = to prepare – put ready. Till, until – to till – all the same word' (*CN* I. 1582). Sadly, they are not the same word. In 1804 he picked up one of Tooke's speculations about the origins of the word 'truth', and created an endearingly illogical series of etymological leaps: 'truth, troweth, throweth i.e. hitteth = itteth = it is *it*' (*CN* II. 2354). A pleasing sequence, but only the first two words have any etymological connection. He was capable of sheer speculation – 'Thousand, derived probably from Thou and Sand' (*CN* I. 456) – though he would make a suggestion for the etymology of 'Dunnage' which may be right: 'any thin thing interposed between goods & the Ship to prevent the former from wet or injury – from *Dun*, thin?' (*CN* II. 2473).

His etymologies depended upon his reading and his amazing memory as well as on the fashions of his particular historical moment, but even the wrong etymologies – sometimes especially the wrong ones – reveal his fascination with how language works and with historical change. A notebook entry drawing heavily on a dictionary and a long letter both show him strenuously attempting to derive the noun 'mind' from the verb 'to mow', with extensive reference to the origins of 'to mow' for which he was, again, indebted to Tooke. He was neither simply following a crazy idea, nor showing off for the sake of his correspondent. Unlike Tooke, he wanted to make the link so as to claim for 'mind' the characteristics of what he thought of as its 'vibratory yet progressive motion'; its ability, like a scythe, 'to move forward & backward, yet still progressively' (*CN* I. 378; *CL* I. 696–8). As in his sequence of five moves from 'truth' to 'it is *it*', he wished to show how the mind operated in the context of the body's needs (and to show it via physical analogies). He had insisted in 1800: 'I would endeavor to destroy the old antithesis of *Words & Things*, elevating, as it were, words into Things, & living Things too' (*CL* I. 626). Late in life, he would claim that 'With the few exceptions of words imitating sound, every word has a primary visual image, as it's proper, at least, it's original sense' (*CL* VI. 700–1).

On New Year's Day 1806, as if promising himself to be as imaginative as possible in the new year, he invented a way of deriving 'thing' from 'to think' which totally reversed Tooke's belief that the noun 'thing' came first:

> Reo = reor [to think] probably an obsolete Latin word, and res the second person singular of the Present Indicative – ... Res = thou art thinking. – Even so our 'Thing': id est, thinking or think'd. Think, Thank, Tank = Reservoir of what has been *thinged* – Denken, Danken – I forget the German for Tank/The, Them, This, These, Thence, Thick, Thing, Thong, Thou, may be all Hocus-pocused by metaphysical Etymology into Brothers and Sisters – with many a Cousin-German ...
>
> (*CN* II. 2784)

Metaphysical etymology indeed. He loved such things not simply because of the bewitching way in which he could hocus-pocus the solutions he wanted. He was thoroughly serious about the way in which 'think' needed to precede 'thing' in the development of human language; the activity of the consciousness and the imagination must come first.

He would set this out playfully in 1809 when suggesting that 'Thought is the participle past of Thing', and that thinking is '*thinging*, or thing out of me', so that 'a thing acts on me but not on me as purely passive'. He is not, so to speak, 'thinged' *by* his experience; he is the one able to 'thing or think' (*CN* III. 3587). To his son Derwent in 1818 he would comment: 'To think ... is to *thingify*' (*CL* IV. 885). In just that way, puns ('best when exquisitely bad' – *CL* I. 295) were pleasing not simply as jokes but because they exposed the primary meanings of words, language itself being 'formed upon associations of this kind' (*CN* III. 3762). Having imagined bankers boasting 'of their Prose-perity', he claimed for himself 'Poetry-perity' and continued: 'Pros-perous and Verse-perus'. He was, a friend recalled, 'never above a pun when it crossed his mind opportunely'; for years he planned an essay 'in defence of Punning'.[6]

Poetry and prose

There is something of a problem with insisting that language needs to be 'natural' (the word gave Coleridge as much trouble as it did any of his contemporaries) while simultaneously seeing it as developing and becoming richer and more complex, with the meaning of a word always including all the associations it recalls. His insistence in *Biographia Literaria*, however, that the finest test of poetic language is its '*untranslatableness*' (*BL* II. 142) reminds us that for him poetry was distinctive for its use of very particular words in very particular places. Late in life, in an off-the-cuff definition of good prose, he would call it 'Proper words in their proper places'; good verse was therefore 'The *most* proper words in the *most* proper places' (*CL* VI. 928).

An example would be the phrase 'secret Ministry' for the unremitting, stealthy activity of frost in Coleridge's poem 'Frost at Midnight' (*CPI* I. 453). That piece would also be a good example of a 'conversation poem' in which, though never a word is spoken aloud (for only one person is awake), the poem concentrates on the ideal surroundings for the sleeping 'cradled infant' at its centre. The narrator suffered a fearsome town education, 'pent 'mid cloisters dim'; the child, however, can expect to 'wander like a breeze / By lake and sandy shores'.

> Therefore all seasons shall be sweet to thee,
> Whether the summer clothe the general earth
> With greenness, or the redbreast sit and sing
> Betwixt the tufts of snow on the bare branch
> Of mossy apple-tree, while the nigh thatch
> Smokes in the sun-thaw . . .   (*CPI* I. 455–6)

The simplicity of the language is something that, without Wordsworth, Coleridge would probably never have adopted. But where Coleridge had originally ended the poem with lines about the infant's perception of glittering icicles that 'make thee shout, / And stretch and flutter from thy mother's arms / As thou would'st fly for very eagerness', he found that those lines 'destroy the rondo, and return upon itself of the Poem' (*CPI* I. 456). He realised that he needed to return to the uncanny 'ministry' of frost and the quietness of the night sky, so that the poem ends:

> . . . whether the eave-drops fall
> Heard only in the trances of the blast,
> Or if the secret ministry of frost

> Shall hang them up in silent icicles,
> Quietly shining to the quiet Moon.
>
> (*CPI* i. 456)

These are things that the poem has made as 'sweet' to us as they are to the growing infant. Coleridge scribbled another definition of poetry into his note-book in 1809: 'poetry demands a *severer keeping* – it admits nothing that Prose may not often admit; but it *oftener* rejects. In other words, it presupposes a more continuous state of Passion' (*CN* iii. 3611).

But Coleridge also ensured that his prose was as well-considered as his poetry. Example after example springs off the pages of his writing: his looking up at a hazy sky at night and observing 'two or three dim untwinkling[7] Stars, like full stops on damp paper'; his observation of 'the convulsive agonies of the Caterpillar in its laborious forth-struggle from the tegument that compressed its wings'; his joyful description, in April 1804, of a fellow-passenger on the *Speedwell* as 'an unconscientiously fat woman, who would have wanted Elbow Room on Salisbury Plain/a body that might have been in a less spendthrift mood of Nature sliced into a company, & a reasonable slice allotted to her as Corporal!' (*CN* i. 1648, iii. 3362, *CL* ii. 1123). 'Unconscientiously' means 'unscrupulously'; Coleridge seems conscientiously to have been avoiding 'unconscionably' (inordinately). And, of course, 'Corporal' contains its own pun.

One of the excitements of reading Coleridge, in consequence, is that of following his ongoing attempt to define and newly refine the operation (and the arrangement in the mind and on the page) of what he once called the 'measured' words that make up language (*CN* iii. 3286).

The natural language of poetry

It was not surprising that when Coleridge and Wordsworth planned their volume of *Lyrical Ballads* in the early summer of 1798, they should have done so not only to publish poems together, but in order to promote a theory or science of language which at this point they believed they shared, however much they came to disagree about it later. Both were, politically, democrats and reformers and they believed that their poetry should, so far as possible, democratise poetry, by adopting 'the language of conversation in the middle and lower classes of society' (*PW* i. 116). The inclusion of Coleridge's 'The Rime of the Ancyent Marinere' in the 1798 collection, with its numerous self-conscious archaisms, might have seemed to go against the spirit and fact of that ideal; but, as their Advertisement explained, the poem was 'written in imitation of the *style*, as well as the spirit of the elder poets; but with a few exceptions, the Author believes that the language adopted in it has been equally intelligible for these three last centuries' (*PW* I. 117). The archaic words were, in one way, a proof of the long tradition of language in which the poem was written; they demonstrated Coleridge's desire to recover 'an older, more authentic mode of discourse' in 'primitive speech-patterns' that were innately 'natural'.[8] And in 1799 Coleridge would, anyway, make it clear that a liking for poetry which gave pleasure because it was 'not perfectly understood' was something he was very happy to have grown out of (*CN* I. 383).

By the second half of September 1800, Wordsworth had developed their few preliminary words about the conversation of the middle and lower classes into a theory of poetic language ('a selection of the real language of men in a state of vivid sensation') which involved such statements as 'there neither is nor can be' any 'essential difference between the language of prose and metrical composition' (*PW* I. 119, 134). The original plan had been for Coleridge to write this Preface, and the notebook he was using late in August 1800 shows him jotting down ideas arising from conversations with Wordsworth; 'recalling of passion in tranquillity', for example, appeared in Coleridge's notebook before Wordsworth penned the phrase 'emotion recollected in tranquillity' (*CN* I. 787 and n.).

However, Coleridge had been unsure about the relationship of 'rustic life' to 'the *best* parts of language' (*BL* II. 40) ever since 1798; and as early as November 1801, he would wonder whether he shouldn't rebel against 'distinct, clear, full made Images', because of the damage they might do to what he called 'the vital & idea-creating force' of poetry (*CN* I. 1016). And by 1808 he was arguing for 'Very different kinds of Style . . . both in different men, & in different parts of the same poem'; language being 'an almost infinite sphere of variety' (*LL* I. 87; *CN* III. 3810). As chapter 6 will show, by the time he wrote *Biographia Literaria* in 1815 Coleridge had grown particularly critical of Wordsworth's 1800 proposition that there was no 'essential difference between the language of prose and metrical composition' (*BL* II. 55); he would for example suggest that 'Language is the sacred Fire in the Temple of Humanity, and the Muses are it's especial & Vestal Priestesses' (*CL* III. 522). Such language demonstrates Coleridge's final, symbolic rejection of the idea of the 'natural'; 'poetry as poetry is essentially *ideal*' (*BL* II. 450), he would declare in 1817.

Copying and coining

Coleridge always believed that, like his father, he would write grammars, dictionaries and lexicons: 'Diction. of hard words' he noted down as a project in

1803, with a couple of immediate candidates in 'defenestrate' and the fascinating substance 'Nostoc'.[9] His notebooks frequently included examples of 'hard words', like 'Mismotion' and 'unapparel' (*CN* I. 1786), both from Donne's poem 'Obsequies to the Lord Harrington'. In one notebook he wrote out the start of a Greek Vocabulary which would be abandoned when he commenced work on *The Friend* in the autumn of 1809; in another notebook he wrote the headings for a brief German grammar, in yet another the start of a Greek grammar (*CN* III. 3422, 4336, IV. 4644). All his life he made copious notes on grammar, metre and language, and at various times collected words that were either obsolete or had changed their meaning (*CN* IV. 4965). The Cumbrian word 'lownded', meaning sheltered, became, for example, part of his everyday vocabulary (*CN* I. 1204, *CL* II. 858). On one occasion, for no obvious reason, he wrote down twenty-nine terms of abuse running from 'fool' to 'fop-doodle' (*CN* III. 3940). He himself employed a huge vocabulary containing (for a man born in 1772) a surprising number of sixteenth- and seventeenth-century words and spellings, for example 'introclude', 'inturbidate', 'comburent', 'harbourous' and 'accrescence' (*CN* II. 2370, III. 3869, 4036, 4043, *CM* IV. 845). The cause was his deep reading in the theology, history and literature of the seventeenth century.

At times, he was persuaded, the right word simply had to be invented, in order to be faithful to the mind's complex experience: 'Words correspond to thoughts' (*CL* VI. 630). In 1808 he inscribed an 'Important Hint' to himself: 'The powers of conscious intellect increase by the accession of an organon [i.e. the means by which some process of thinking is carried out] or new word' (*CN* III. 3268). When young, he had often been extravagant rather than thoughtful in his inventions, and had accepted criticisms made, for example, of the 'affectation of double Epithets' in his early poems, 'the component parts of which are indebted for their union exclusively to the printer's hyphen' (*SWF* I. 302). He also agreed with the criticism that words like 'Unshuddered' and 'unaghasted' were 'indeed truely ridiculous' (*CL* I. 215). A man who attended his May 1808 lectures on poetry, however, recalled the start of one lecture:

> When Coleridge came into the Box there were several Books laying. He opened two or three of them silently and shut them again after a short inspection. He then paused, & leaned His head on His hand, and at last said, He had been thinking for a word to express the distinct character of Milton as a Poet, but not finding one that wd. express it, He should make one '*Ideality*'. He spoke extempore. – (*LL* I. 145 and nn. 11–12)

The word dates from 1700 but Coleridge seems to have been the first person to employ it in the *OED* sense of 'The faculty or capacity of conceiving ideals; the imaginative faculty'. This is a truly Coleridgian definition: yet another attempt to describe what goes on in the mind of a poet, another exploration of the interactive processes of human reason and imagination.

It is also remarkable how often Coleridge picked up on new words and usages dating from the late eighteenth century and employed them himself; the *OED* cites him as the first user of a number of key words for which he was not in fact responsible, but which he may have helped establish. One could cite, just from his lifetime, 'bathetic' (from 1799), 'colloquialism' (from 1796), 'humanism' (from 1776), 'intellectualize' (from 1792), 'psychological' (from 1776) and 'realism' (from 1797). All were new words of which he realised the significance (he may well have discovered 'Realismus' in Kant or one of his followers). He would, however, react against William Sotheby's use of the wholly literary word 'lone' in his tragedy *Orestes*, wondering 'if indeed it be a word at all, and not a mere Birmingham [i.e. manufacture] of poetic convenience' (*SWF* I. 120).

He was, too, thoroughly conversant with the languages of science. He suggested to Humphry Davy various names for chemical substances and compounds, and was responsible for the noun 'substrate' (*CN* II. 3192); he also kept up-to-date in the language of scientific discovery, referring in 1810 to potassium (first named in 1807) and in 1816 to titanium (discovered 1796), osmium (discovered 1803) and platinum, first named as such in 1812.[10] He was also the only non-scientific writer who ever appears to have employed the medical term 'introition' (*CN* I. 1616), first used in 1762 to describe how fluid enters a cavity of the body; being Coleridge, he used it figuratively to describe how his son Hartley entered on the experience of nature. His awareness of language in history, geography and literature demonstrates itself everywhere; he noted in 1822 that Neapolitans were 'degenerate in the original sense of the word, De genere – they have lost their race' (*CN* IV. 4866), and in 1809 he appears to have been the first person since Tobias Smollett's *Roderick Random* (1771) – a novel he loved – to use the word 'housemate' (*Friend* II. 28).

He was also very conscious of how 'new things necessitate new terms' (*Friend* I. 449) and he coined words himself, in large numbers. His 1825 religious work *Aids to Reflection*, for example, would bring some sixty new words or usages into the English language,[11] and over his lifetime he was responsible for many more. Sometimes he simply translated a word from French or Latin or Greek or German and a new English word came into existence. 'Technique' was such a word; first used by Coleridge in 1817. It is astonishing to imagine that it had never been used in English before, but the French 'la technique' was there and Coleridge playfully transposed it, though the word was not picked up and used again until the 1870s.

'Forget-me-not' was such another. Seventeenth-century herbalists had used the name for the small blue flower which in German is called *Vergissmeinnicht*; Coleridge in effect returned 'Forget-me-not' to common English speech with the publication in 1817 of his poem 'The Keep-Sake' and his prominent note: 'One of the names (and meriting to be the only one) of the *Myosotis Scorpioides Palustris*; a flower from six to twelve inches high, with blue blossom and bright yellow eye' (*CPI* ii. 710).

He also consciously created words not just to correspond to new experience, but because he felt it incumbent on him, as literary and philosophical pioneer, to do so. 'Men of great Genius find in new words & new combinations the sin that most easily besets them/a strong feeling of originality seems to receive a gratification by new Terms' (*CN* i. 1835). Developing language was a cheerful and deliberate process to him, and one he was happy to fantasise about in his notebook in 1807:

> O for the power to persuade all the writers of G. B. to adopt the ver, zer, and ab of the German – why not verboil, zerboil? versend, zersend? I should like the very words verflossen, zerflossen, to be naturalized – and as I look,
>
>> now feels my Soul creative Throes,
>> And now all Joy, all sense, Zerflows.
>
> I do not know, whether I am in earnest, or in sport, while I recommend this Ver & Zer...[12]

It was both a game *and* serious, though he had no luck in getting such prefixes into English. He was less serious when describing miniature cataracts as 'little dancing Kittenracts' (*CN* i. 415; see too iv. 4927). No one ever followed him and the *OED* ignores the word.

Coleridge was nevertheless a person of enormous responsive and imaginative power and his memory and his vocabulary were astonishing. On numerous occasions while writing this book, I have felt obliged to check his language in the dictionary; never in my life have I engaged with a writer with such a vocabulary, such a habit of playing with existing language and such a delight in creating new forms of the obscurest words. Not only did he know the word 'revomit' but he happily coined a noun from it: 'Is the Dog, who has licked up his Gorge, secure from revomition?' (*CN* i. 695). Even the word 'Gorge' – 'What has been swallowed, the contents of the stomach...primarily of *Falconry*' (*OED*) – was rare after the seventeenth century. In the notebook in which he recorded his tour of Scotland in 1803, he used the word '*precipicy*' as an adjective from 'precipice'; two pages later he used the word 'floatage' to describe the shadows on the surface of a stream (*CN* I. 1489). Which was the invention, which the old word? ('*Precipicy*' was his invention; 'floatage' – as 'flotage' – had been recorded in 1672.)

And although he deplored the use of unusual words as 'ridiculous in the topics of ordinary conversation', he hugely enjoyed the *play* of language and what one could do with one's linguistic resources (*Friend* I. 449). He told Poole in 1796 that he wanted a servant-girl 'scientific in vaccimulgence [i.e. milking cows] . . . That last word is a new one; but soft in sound, and full of expression. Vaccimulgence! – I am pleased with the word' (*CL* I. 251). Writing to Davy in 1800, he happily fantasised how 'with what an athanasiophagous Grin we shall march together – we *poets*: Down with all the rest of the World! – By the word athanasiophagous I mean devouring Immortality by anticipation – 'Tis a sweet Word! –' (*CL* I. 557). Having found 'egomism' in the eighteenth-century metaphysician Andrew Baxter (who had taken it from the French to mean 'The belief of one who considers himself the only being in existence'), Coleridge developed 'Egomist' (*CN* I. 174 and n.), a coinage never re-used by anyone; so that in spite of its predating 'solipsist' by eighty years or so, it died seconds after its first inscription. Finally, he invented 'marginalia': especially appropriate for him as one of the great writers in margins. Before Coleridge, the noun had been 'marginal', meaning 'A marginal note, reference, or decoration' (*OED*); examples would be the printed 'marginals' which he himself supplied for his 1817 'Ancient Mariner'.

The older he got, the less he stuck to his own rule of avoiding the unusual in language; words gave him too much pleasure. His later letters are peppered with words like 'centrifugations', 'Desquamation' and 'incondite', while we find him in 1818 happily creating the sentence: 'His lands deglabrate not to say deglupt, and his last resources degrandescent and degumiated' (*CL* VI. 813, 927, 939, *CN* III. 4425) – one obsolete and three invented words. A man listening to him talk in the 1820s was irritated by his 'using words in a sense not familiar to me' (*TT* I. lxxiii), but Coleridge never lost the taste for linguistic play, as when in December 1829 he called some Christmas sausages 'supershoppic', meaning 'superior to shop-bought', and noted a fortnight later a 'snow-frozen boy-slidden Hill' (*CN* V. 6229, 6245).

Language's debt to Coleridge

We need only to consult a dictionary or database which records first usages to find ourselves amazed at how much Coleridge did for the English language. He had in his lifetime argued for the desirability of a dictionary constructed on historical principles, one which, 'regarding words as living growths, offlets, and organs of the human soul, seeks to trace each historically' (*Logic* 126). The *Oxford English Dictionary* is that very dictionary, so it is appropriate that it should so frequently cite him; often as the inventor of words, sometimes their translator, sometimes their adapter, sometimes their populariser.[13] I have already mentioned some of the words he formed; we can add 'offlet' from his sentence about what an historical dictionary should contain. A great stack of other words might be added; the figure is in the hundreds. A further brief list of his first usages, none previously mentioned, might contain

> actualise, bisexual, bulgy, factual, intensify, Messianic, multivocal, Narcissism, neuropathology, phenomenal, productivity, psychoanalytical, psychosomatic, refuel, rehouse, relativity, reliability, romanticise, subjectivity, telegraph-pole, uniqueness, unpublishable, unrecognisable, unreliable, visualise

He would have smiled wryly at the fact that he should have bequeathed both 'unpublishable' and 'unreliable' to us, but (two centuries on) it would seem impossible to write in English without being indebted to him.

Criticism

Although he had helped Wordsworth write the prefaces for *Lyrical Ballads* in 1798 and 1800, and had also done some reviewing early in life, Coleridge first became famous as a critic because of the lecturing he did between 1808 and 1819. He eventually gave over seventy lectures on literary subjects, mostly in London and Bristol; the most famous were the eighteen or twenty lectures he gave in London between January and June 1808, on 'The Principles of Poetry' (in which he paid some attention to Shakespeare's plays), twelve lectures on Shakespeare and Milton given in London between November 1811 and January 1812, and finally ten more, mostly on Shakespeare, in London 1818–19.

Shakespeare lectures

In his stress on Shakespeare's judgement and intelligence in his 1811–12 series, Coleridge would be accused of plagiarising the German Shakespeare scholar August Wilhelm von Schlegel. In praising the intelligence of Shakespeare rather than his instinct, during his 1808 lecture series, he may, however, have coincided with (rather than have followed) Schlegel. It was at any rate a noteworthy moment for Shakespeare criticism, which had always tended to fall back on the notion of Shakespeare as untutored, *natural* genius. To have two of the great European intellectuals of the early nineteenth century insisting that Shakespeare possessed 'a philosophic mind and power of judgement' (*LL* I. 20) was a radical development in Shakespeare studies.

We do not, however, have much evidence of how Coleridge actually framed such an insight. Wordsworth, for example, heard Coleridge's last two lectures on Shakespeare in 1812, but four years later would write as if the eighteenth century's attitude to Shakespeare as a natural genius remained unchallenged; either he had forgotten what Coleridge had said, had missed the point, or (more likely) Coleridge's defence of Shakespeare's intelligence had played only a small part in his lectures. It does not appear in the surviving notes Coleridge made for what he would say, so may well have been an extempore addition. As with so much in these literary lectures, what Coleridge actually said remains rather obscure, though the reputation he gained – and conferred – was hugely important.

The lecture he gave on 2 January 1812, for instance, the twelfth of the second series, assisted in shaping discussion of *Hamlet* for the next 150 years. The lecture contained a series of reflections on action and procrastination which meant that the play came to be seen as dealing with profound ideas, having previously been regarded as rather old-fashioned and incoherent. Because of Coleridge's 'Philosophical criticism' (*LL* II. 293) the character of Hamlet in particular came, for the first time, to be seen as an object for intellectual investigation. Dr Johnson had argued less than fifty years earlier that Hamlet's refusal to kill the praying king (because the act might dispatch him to heaven) was 'too horrible to be read or to be uttered'.[1] Coleridge's Hamlet is a very different character. Burdened as he is by feelings of 'reluctance and procrastination', Hamlet according to Coleridge talks himself out of killing the king only because he wants a 'pretext for not acting' (*LL* II. 354, 458). Hamlet is, however, distinguished above all other Shakespearean characters by 'enormous intellectual activity' (*LL* I. 539).

In spite of his plans and promises, Coleridge never managed to get a book – nor even a single published essay – out of any of his Shakespeare lectures, for the simple reason that he never even tried to write them down. He had discovered in 1808 that he spoke most fluently when improvising; he would talk for up to an hour and a half, relying on some notes, a book or two, his wonderful memory and his incredible range of reading. All that survives of what he prepared for his Shakespeare lectures are some scattered notes and the markings he made in various copies of the plays; in some cases extensive comments, in other cases very brief remarks. At times in his lectures he drew directly upon such materials, but at other times positively ignored them. And for many of his lectures not even notes or marked copies survive (nothing exists for the 2 January 1812 lecture, for example). As a result, the only access possible to Coleridge's famous *Hamlet* lecture is through the accounts written by people who were present. For his 1813 lecture some notes survive in the copy of a copy made by his great-nephew, and for the 1819 lectures we at least have his marked-up copy of the plays.

Between 1836 and 1839, revised and partly rewritten versions of some of his surviving notes, amalgamated with press reports of the lectures (and no distinction made between the two), were published. In 1856, furthermore, fully written-out versions appeared of shorthand notes taken down during seven of the 1811–12 lectures by the writer and critic John Payne Collier. By the 1880s, a mass of apparently authentic Coleridge critical and lecture material was in print in Thomas Ashe's *Coleridge's Lectures and Notes on Shakspere and Other English Poets* (1883). Few readers seem to have realised that the lecture texts depended on press reports and shorthand notes written up after the event by those who had been present.

In particular, the 1812 lecture material (including the famous *Hamlet* lecture) is suspect. Everything we know of Collier, his shorthand system and the way he later wrote up his texts, shows that while the general ideas are Coleridge's, the particular expressions will be so only occasionally. It is easy to establish how unreliable Collier is. In the second lecture of the series, where Coleridge's own notes show that in discussing the word 'virtue' he wished to refer to 'manly strength' and 'Moral Excellence', Collier's shorthand produced 'merely strength' and 'modern excellence' (*LL* i. 202, 204). When Collier in 1856 turned his shorthand into a more complete version of the 2 January 1812 lecture, he stressed Hamlet's 'endless reasoning and hesitating – constant urging and solicitation of the mind to act, and as constant an escape from action; ceaseless reproaches of himself for sloth and negligence, while the whole energy of his resolution evaporates in these reproaches.' This behaviour is 'from that aversion to action, which prevails among such as have a world in themselves' (*LL* ii. 537). Collier ends up with the ringing conclusion that Hamlet is a man 'called upon to act by every motive human and divine, but the great object of his life is defeated by continually resolving to do, yet doing nothing but resolve' (*LL* ii. 541).

If we compare this with what Collier actually took down in shorthand in 1812, a very different text emerges. Hamlet, in the rather incoherent shorthand, suffers 'endless reasoning perpetual solicitation of the mind to act but as constant escapes from action   Reproaches of himself for his sloth yet the whole energy passing away in these reproaches . . . merely from the aversion to action of those who have a world in themselves' (*LL* ii. 456). Not a word appears of the famous conclusion about 'continually resolving'. It was created by Collier when he rewrote the lecture in 1856.

The fundamental problem with Collier's transcriptions is that he was making a link between Coleridge and Hamlet and would consciously (or unconsciously) have ensured that his recollection of what Coleridge had said in his lectures conformed to what he believed to be true about Coleridge. When we come across those famous formulations about Hamlet, we need to ask who is commenting on whom. The same applies to one of the most famous remarks Coleridge is ever supposed to have made: 'I have a smack of Hamlet myself, if I may say so' (*TT* ii. 61). His nephew Henry Nelson Coleridge, who was with Coleridge on 24 June 1827 and included this remark in his 1835 collection of Coleridge's *Table Talk*, confessed that he had made no notes at the time: 'I could not for two or three days afterwards . . . put any thing on paper' (*TT* ii. 60, i. xcii, 76–7 n. 22). Nor did he include the remark when he eventually came to write up the day's talk. It first appeared in his 1835 edition; its authenticity is thus rather doubtful. The lecture texts are equally dubious and yet they remain widely quoted as Coleridge's own words.[2]

In the case of a writer like Coleridge, for whom the exact word was so important, and so often pondered over, weaknesses in the texts of the lectures (newspaper reports and Collier's versions) should rule them out of serious critical discussion. Not being entirely by Coleridge, they are also often extremely dull. All I can do is recommend that readers stick to the passages about poetry and writers which survive in Coleridge's notes and marked-up copies (included in *LL*), his notebooks (*CN*), his letters (*CL*), and his marginalia (*CM*). Only those allow the reader access to the words that Coleridge actually used.

Other Shakespeare criticism

More notable are some of Coleridge's individual local comments about Shakespeare's texts. It was Coleridge who, in 1817, invented the phrase 'practical criticism', and he was the first critic to go beyond using critical comment as purely moral or textual commentary. Some of the comments he wrote into his Shakespeare editions on the exchanges between Polonius and Reynaldo, and then between Polonius and Ophelia, are psychologically acute:

> no wonder . . . if that which can be *put down by rule* in the memory
> should appear mere poring, maudlin-eyed Cunning, slyness blinking
> thro' the watry eye of superannuation. So in this admirable Scene.
> Polonius, who is throughout the Skeleton of his own former Skill and
> State-craft, hunts the trail of policy at a dead scent, supplied by the weak
> fever-smell in his own nostrils. – (*LL* ii. 300)

'At a dead scent' means 'when the scent has gone cold' (Coleridge is thinking of 'He is now at a cold scent' from *Twelfth Night*). Again, he is astute
in his comments on Polonius's offer to hide behind the arras, commenting
that 'Polonius's volunteer obtrusion of himself into this business' is 'appropriate to his character still letching [i.e. longing] after former importance'. The
language of the play-within-a-play is, Coleridge suggests, 'lyric vehemence
and epic pomp', creating a 'contrast between Hamlet & the play of Hamlet –'
(*LL* i. 542). Claudius's prayer ends 'All may be well!'; Coleridge notes the
'degree of Merit attributed by the self-flattering Soul to its own struggle'
(*LL* ii. 353). About Hamlet himself, he writes: 'Hamlet's madness is made
to consist in the full utterance of all the thoughts that had past thro' his mind
before – in telling home truths', while on Hamlet's saying to his mother, about
his father's death, 'Ay madam, it is common', Coleridge comments 'Suppression
prepares for overflow –' (*LL* ii. 354, 298).

   He is equally acute about *Othello*. Lines from Othello's last speech ('Like
the base Indian, threw a pearl away / Richer than all his tribe') elicit this
note: 'Othello wishes to excuse himself on the score of ignorance; & yet not
to excuse himself – to excuse himself by accusing. This struggle of feeling is
finely conveyed in the word 'base' which is applied to the rude Indian not in his
own character, but as a momentary representative of Othello's' (*CM* iv. 748).
Finally, he finds an admirable way of suggesting what it is like to be watching,
or reading, a Shakespeare text; he demonstrates its characteristic combination
of psychological and linguistic naturalness. 'If I should not speak it, I feel that
I should be thinking it – the voice only is the Poet's, the words are my own'
(*LL* ii. 139).

   These marked-up copies, together with Coleridge's own surviving notes, at
least supply us with the language he used when writing about Shakespeare.

Criticism in notebooks and marginalia

Coleridge's comments on literature in general, although fragmentary, are rich
and surprising. He was an excellent reader of other people's poetry and acute in
his comments. When, for example, John Thelwall showed him his own poems
in October 1797, Coleridge waved away the fact that one of them, calling itself
a sonnet, was a twenty-five-line poem in blank verse. He did, however, note
that 'the epithet "downy" is probably more applicable to Susan's upper lip than
to her Bosom', and helpfully advised his wordy friend to '*Study compression!*'
(*CL* i. 351). Very few people of Coleridge's generation had any time for the

poetry of John Donne. Coleridge, however, read difficult poems like 'A Vale-diction Forbidding Mourning' with delight; it is 'An admirable Poem which none but D. could have written. Nothing were ever more admirably made out than the figure of the Compass. –'. He noted about lines from 'The Good-Morrow': 'Too good for mere wit. It contains a deep practical truth – this Triplet'; and he commented: 'To read Dryden, Pope &c, you need only count syllables; but to read Donne you must measure *Time*...' (*CM* II. 223, 218, 216). These comments, all made after 1811, appear in marginalia in a 1669 copy of Donne belonging to Charles Lamb, who encouraged people to lend Coleridge their books on the grounds that 'he will return them... enriched with annotations, tripling their value' (*CL* III. 55 n.). The fact that Coleridge's surviving marginalia now occupy six fat printed volumes suggests the range of work he annotated, and what energy of thought went into this unusual form of literary (and theological, historical and scientific) criticism. The marginalia are typically Coleridgian in that they originally represented an individual voice speaking in the privacy of its own study, without any real prospect of reaching other readers – except in so far as any comment and criticism is an invitation to those who come after to engage with it. And Coleridge was perfectly right to trust that later readers would respond.

In the same way, he read Marvell and Herbert, and annotated his own contemporaries' work. He quoted the whole of 'Lines to Mrs Unwin', a poem by Cowper of which he was very fond, and in the course of a long notebook entry discussed what was good and what was weak about it; he then added a commentary suggesting the transposition and omission of certain stanzas that would still better preserve the '*real*ness' of the poem (*CN* II. 2433). He copied out pages of his friend John Hookham Frere's unpublished translation of Aristophanes' play *The Frogs*, with comments, and in 1810 he developed some lengthy criticisms of Scott's 'The Lady of the Lake' which demonstrated his own belief 'how little instructive any criticism can be which does not enter into minutiae' (*CN* III. 4331–2, 3970).

It was occasionally possible for Coleridge to be not just a critical reader but a participant. We have far too little evidence about the ways he influenced Wordsworth's work, but in a few cases details survive. In 1798, Wordsworth much later recalled, he had been wondering about a 'prefatory stanza' for his poem 'We are Seven', and had said to Coleridge '"I should sit down to our little tea-meal with greater pleasure if my task was finished."' He 'mentioned in substance' the kind of thing he wanted, 'and Coleridge immediately threw off the stanza'.[3] Coleridge's sheer facility was always a matter of wonderment to Wordsworth. Sometime late in 1806 or early in 1807, while reading the

1805 version of Wordsworth's *Prelude*, Coleridge found lines which summed up Wordsworth's experience at Trinity College, Cambridge:

> An open slight
> Of College cares and study was the scheme,
> Nor entertain'd without concern for those
> To whom my worldly interests were dear . . .

Coleridge thought the passage awkwardly compressed; Wordsworth's later, revised version ends:

> Nor had, in truth, the scheme been *formed by me*
> *Without uneasy forethought of the pain,*
> *The censures, and ill-omening of those*
> To whom my worldly interests were dear.[4]

The words in italics were all written by Coleridge, who had not only argued that the passage needed expansion, but had engaged in that rarest of all criticisms, the truly practical one; he had written alternative lines from which Wordsworth was able to select.

Of all the writers Coleridge valued, Milton must take first place. Coleridge's homage took many forms. In 1794, he introduced into poetry the word 'scathing' as an adjective for the searing destructiveness of lightning; he took it from Milton's verb 'scathe' in *Paradise Lost*.[5] Coleridge not only annotated texts but filled his notebooks with quotations. Reading Milton's *Of Reformation* in 1796, for example, he made a brief entry in his notebook containing three quotations he relished: 'a paroxysm of citations', 'pampered metaphors', 'aphorisming Pedantry' (*CN* I. 108). He fantasised a multi-media experience: 'To have a continued Dream, representing visually & audibly all Milton's Paradise Lost' (*CN* I. 658). He also planned a poem about him: 'Milton, a Monody in the metres of Samson's Choruses – only with more rhymes/ – poetical influences – political – moral' (*CN* I. 1155). Coleridge's continuing love of Milton (not just the poetry but the prose work) was also one of the signs of his own continuing radicalism; as late as 1809, he thought works like 'Milton's proposals for Toleration in Religion, Liberty of the Press, &c.' (*CN* III. 3590) necessary to the intelligent organisation of society. The title of his first lecture series, in 1808, gave Milton a place beside Shakespeare, even if, in the event, Coleridge did not say much about him; in his introductory Milton lecture, on 6 May, 'the word poetry was not used till the lecture was two-thirds over, nor Milton's name till ten minutes before the close' (*LL* I. 114). Some notebook entries all the same supply us with an idea of what he would have wanted to say; he cited Milton's creation 'in three incidental words' ('simple, sensuous, and passionate') of what he called a 'strictly adequate definition' of poetry (*CN* III. 3287, 3615). Definitions, like distinctions between words, were always subjects of fascination for him.

It was indeed the passionate quality of language which Coleridge always thought that Wordsworth should have stressed in his published statements about poetry, rather than the way a poet's language should be related to everyday speech. Coleridge would praise Wordsworth's best poetry for its 'impassioned, lofty, and sustained diction' and its employment of 'the natural language of empassioned feeling' (*BL* II. 8, 41). The passion and excitement in Wordsworth's work were what he chose to discuss in the only non-theological prose book of his life, dictated to J. J. Morgan in 1815 – *Biographia Literaria*.

Biographia Literaria

Coleridge had thought about such a book and planned it (and changed his mind about it) for years; back in 1803, he had thought of writing his 'metaphysical works' in the form of an autobiography, 'intermixed with all the other events or history of the mind & fortunes of S. T. Coleridge' (*CN* I. 1515). It was a characteristically original idea, and also characteristic that he should not have got around to it for another twelve years. From the start it sounded potentially a prey to muddle and oddity, 'intermixed' as the theoretical writing would be with all those other events. The *Biographia* took up Coleridge's old idea of a treatise on aesthetics, in particular an enquiry into the nature of poetry, that would bring together his interests in religion, psychology, philosophy and literature so as to show them operating in his own mind – and in Wordsworth's poetry.

The project had, however, actually started life as a preface planned for a book bringing together his own scattered poems; he had mentioned such an idea in 1809, and again in 1811 (*Friend* I. 36, *CL* III. 324), and had suggested that he might also discuss Wordsworth and Southey in the preface. When he started to dictate the *Biographia* in June 1815, it came as part of a new and desperate determination, with the help of the Morgans, to set his literary affairs in order. In 1815, however, he was also aware of how, ever since *Lyrical Ballads* in 1798, Wordsworth had fronted *his* volumes of poetry with prefaces. In 1800 had come the preface which they had discussed together and at the end of April 1815, so just two months earlier, Wordsworth's *Poems* had appeared in two volumes with a brand new preface, including certain distinctions between 'Fancy' and 'Imagination'; a distinction which Coleridge would have regarded as his own to make. He wrote to Wordsworth on 30 May 1815, only mentioning in passing Wordsworth's recent 'two Volumes of Poems' but explaining how disappointed he had been with *The Excursion* the previous year because it was *not* the great philosophical poem he had always hoped it would be; but he also announced a preface to his own forthcoming poems, 'which I shall have done in two or at furthest three days' (*CL* IV. 576).

Coleridge's own planned preface, however, transmogrified over a period of months into a piece of writing that no longer introduced his poems but became a work designed to stand alongside them; he hoped (like Wordsworth) to have volumes of poetry and prose appear in 1815. Coleridge's prose volume would, however, also discuss his lifelong intellectual effort, in two quite distinct ways.

He took his chance to tell parts of his life story in the *Biographia*; individual anecdotes about his life and literary dealings are dotted through the work, which was rather misleadingly subtitled 'Biographical Sketches of my Literary Life and Opinions', as if it were still primarily the autobiography he had originally planned (*CL* IV. 585). His accounts of his own early writing career are both frustrating and illuminating. He is unable to recall dates with any accuracy (he gets the publication date of his own first book wrong by two years) and he ignores publications which don't fit the general point he now wants to make. For instance, his own third book (published in 1798) spoils his argument that he has not published anything over his own name since 1796, so he chooses to forget it. On the other hand, he is startlingly frank about himself, describing in chapter II his 'constitutional indolence, aggravated into languor by ill-health; the accumulating embarrassments of procrastination; the mental cowardice, which is the inseparable companion of procrastination, and which makes us anxious to think and converse on any thing rather than on what concerns ourselves' (*BL* I. 44–5). This is more psychologically revealing than almost anything written about him. It coincides exactly with what Dorothy Wordsworth had noticed during his unhappy stay with the Wordsworth family 1809–10: that when Coleridge talked, it was always 'upon subjects as far aloof from himself or his friends as possible' (*LW* II. 1. 399).

What, however, is most compelling about these autobiographical reminiscences is that they keep returning to his relationship with Wordsworth. To no other parts of his life do his 'Biographical Sketches' return so insistently as to the years 1797 and 1798. Anecdote after anecdote, reminiscence after reminiscence, build up a picture of his relationship with Wordsworth, with barely a critical word about the other man but praise a-plenty for his poetry. It would have taken a very sharp-eyed reader to notice a few revealing details; for example, an extract from Pliny which Coleridge had used in *The Friend* in 1809 to praise Wordsworth is here used instead to praise Coleridge's even earlier literary hero, the poet William Bowles (*Friend* II. 108, *BL* I. 12–13). But during chapters I–IV, the creative partnership with Wordsworth serves as the book's focus.

There is one exception; chapter III includes a long encomium on Southey. Coleridge felt deeply indebted to his one-time friend for all he had done for him (and for his children) and now attempted to repay the debt with a series of compliments. It was however rather odd for him to have included such a passage, as it was prefaced by a long footnote explaining that there was really nothing to justify the long-standing journalistic assumption of the existence of a school of Lake Poets made up of Southey, Wordsworth and Coleridge. Such confusion is, however, typical of what happens in the *Biographia*. After that excursion, the book goes back to its concentration on what Coleridge described at the end of the book as 'the first dawn of my literary life' (*BL* II. 159).

The attack on Wordsworth

In July 1802, Coleridge had told a friend that he and Wordsworth had started to have 'some little controversy' about poetic language and they had begun to suspect that there was, 'somewhere or other, a *radical* Difference' (*CL* II. 812) between them, though Coleridge was still sure that they agreed about far more than they disagreed. During the following years, he had gone on praising his friend's poetic endeavours. He had written his poem 'To William Wordsworth' in January 1807 after hearing parts of *The Prelude* read aloud, and he had included extracts from *The Prelude* in *The Friend* in October and December 1809; the first publication of any portion of it.[6]

But their horrible personal quarrel in 1810–11 had led Coleridge to feel that there was now an unbridgeable gulf between him, Wordsworth and those early days. He said little publicly, but I quoted above some of the vicious comments he added to his notebooks. Even after the theoretical reconciliation in which both participated in 1812, Coleridge never felt the same again about Wordsworth. He started what looks like a process of deliberate distancing in May 1815 when he dispatched that devastating letter criticising Wordsworth for *not* having made *The Excursion* 'a *Philosophical Poem*' (*CL* IV. 574), the great work which Coleridge had been expecting all these years (and which he spent pages of his letter outlining and detailing). That would have been excruciating enough for Wordsworth, but he could have had no idea what would come next; a book not just centred upon his friendship with Coleridge, but with serious criticisms of his own principles and practice.

One way of judging the criticism of Wordsworth in *Biographia* is to view it as Coleridge's attempt to redress the balance of a lifetime's admiration. There is external and internal support for such a conclusion. It was striking that, when making arrangements in 1815 with his printers for what at this stage he still thought would be a volume of prefatory remarks to a volume of his poetry, Coleridge had one central stipulation. Morgan, his amanuensis, sent two letters about it, three days apart. 'C: wishes it printed in the size of Wordsworth's last edition. of Poems &c. the prefatory remarks same sized type . . . The preface to these 2 volumes . . . is the one he has fixed on as a prototype for his preface' (*BL* ii. 283–4). Coleridge was making every effort to put his own two-volume publication on exactly the same footing as Wordsworth's; one publication was explicitly designed to match the other.

Although a later chapter starts in the same way as the first four chapters had gone on, with yet another reminiscence of 'the first year that Mr. Wordsworth and I were neighbours' (*BL* ii. 5), Coleridge knew very well that what he would be saying about Wordsworth's poetry and poetic theory would give offence. 'I fear, that my reasonings may not please Wordsworth; but I am convinced, that a detection of the faults in his Poetry is indispensable to a rational appreciation of his merits' (*CL* iv. 591). If there was one thing he would have known about Wordsworth, it was that he took criticism very hard; unlike Coleridge, who argued back when he felt he should, but was also responsive to comments made about his own work. He 'severely criticizes his own productions', noted a friend, who also noticed how Coleridge could not 'be put out of temper'[7] during academic disputes at Göttingen in 1799.

It must have been terribly distressing to Wordsworth to have Coleridge, after all these years of unconditional support, come out with savage criticisms of his writing about poetry *and* of his poetry. In the *Biographia*, however, Coleridge started to dissect not only the ideas of 'Fancy' and 'Imagination' which had appeared so grandly in Wordsworth's Preface to his poems in 1815 (which in Coleridge's analysis quickly come to seem utterly muddled) but also the theory of poetic language Wordsworth had developed back in the late summer of 1800. After a couple of chapters praising Shakespeare (and incidentally using a poem by Wordsworth to bring one chapter to a resounding conclusion), a series of five chapters set out to concentrate explicitly on Wordsworth's poetry and poetic theory. One can hear the knives being sharpened in the list of intended contents:

> *Examination of the tenets peculiar to Mr. Wordsworth – Rustic life (above all,* low *and rustic life) especially unfavorable to the formation of a human diction – The* best *parts of language the product of philosophers, not clowns or shepherds . . .*   (*BL* ii. 40)

Another list would be equally blunt:

> *The characteristic defects of Wordsworth's poetry, with the principles*
> *from which the judgement, that they are defects, is deduced – Their*
> *proportion to the beauties – For the greatest part characteristic of his*
> *theory only . . .   (BL* ii. 119)

Coleridge deals brusquely with the thorny old issue of the language of 'low and rustic life' being appropriate for poetry, the claim made in the 1798 and 1800 Prefaces to *Lyrical Ballads*. Such language, Coleridge now says, can only ever be appropriate for certain kinds of poetry and 'as a *rule*', even for those, 'it is useless, if not injurious, and therefore either need not or ought not to be practised' (*BL* ii. 42). At one stroke, one of Wordsworth's great central claims about the language of poetry is knocked flying. Later in the chapter, and in the following three, more of Wordsworth's resonant phrases about his poetry using the 'real language of men', and about there being no essential difference between the languages of prose and verse, are demolished. That such beliefs are assigned to '*clowns* [i.e. uncouth peasants]' and '*shepherds*' (which would Wordsworth have preferred to be?) is still more offensive; while it is '*philosophers*' who use language better – and which self-proclaimed philosopher had recently been accusing Wordsworth of failing to write philosophical poetry?

Coleridge's brief descriptions of the actual poems also demonstrate, over and over again, that Wordsworth had not actually done what the 1800 Preface had claimed. For Coleridge, Wordsworth's best poetry had never corresponded to his vague theories about language and the rustic life, only those poems which every reader felt were 'sudden and unpleasant sinkings from the height to which the poet had previously lifted them' (*BL* ii. 52). Coleridge's argument also suggests that people in towns feel just as much and use language just as well as people in the country – and that attack was being voiced by a man who had once, because of his loyalty to his friend, gone to live in the Lake District but who had now settled decisively in town.

These attacks, over the five chapters specifically devoted to Wordsworth in the *Biographia*, would have been still more painful because, in his recently published 1815 version of his Preface, Wordsworth had said not a word about rustic language or the real language of men. True, he had included the old Preface at the end of the second volume of his 1815 *Poems*, but the new Preface and the 'Supplementary Essay' written for the 1815 edition hardly address the subject of language at all; one of the few statements that either makes on the subject is that language is 'a thing subject to endless fluctuations and arbitrary associations' (*PW* iii. 82). Coleridge was attacking an old and (for Wordsworth) historic set of ideals; but, in so doing, he was also aligning himself with the savage series of attacks on Wordsworth's poetry made over the years by Francis Jeffrey and the *Edinburgh Review*, which had always sneered at the folly of the 'rustic' in Wordsworth's poetry. Jeffrey had referred in 1807 to the way in which Wordsworth wrote 'upon principle and system' (*BL* i. 71 n. 1); more recently, the *Edinburgh* had described as 'rubbish' the poetry heaped around the occasional good line in *The Excursion*, with the reviewer referring slightingly to Wordsworth's 'peculiar system' (*BL* ii. 115 nn. 3 and 4). And that was a relatively restrained review. Coleridge now employed the same word 'system' about Wordsworth's writing that the *Edinburgh* had used, referring to the 'actual limitations of his system' and remarking how 'groundless does this system appear on a close examination' (*BL* ii. 89).

Even though Coleridge would also attack the *Edinburgh* for its comments on Wordsworth (*BL* i. 113–14), there was no more obvious way for him to demonstrate that he had abandoned any part he might once have played in Wordsworth's enterprise. Reviews of *Biographia Literaria* gleefully singled out his criticisms of Wordsworth and referred to his 'exposure of the hollowness of Mr. W.'s poetical reputation'.[8]

The irony would be that, when Coleridge's major attack on Wordsworth's 1798 and 1800 positions was published, it would come sandwiched between the first publication (in 1816 and 1817) of two of the poems which would make Coleridge's reputation as a poet, 'Kubla Khan' and 'Christabel', both written under the influence of Wordsworth and both written before 1800. To publish a dismissal of Wordsworth's theory *now* was, nevertheless, to loosen the bonds of friendship and alliance whose formation and growth the first part of the book had so carefully established.

Coleridge also had reasons for doing so beyond an attempt to redress an old imbalance. Wordsworth's canard about prose and verse allowed Coleridge to spend time on some favourite subjects – metric and poetic rules – in the course of which he was able to survey a wide range of poetry (Spenser, Daniel, Donne, Cowley, Milton) beside Wordsworth's. More successfully than he had managed in *The Friend*, he had found a public voice; dictating to Morgan had liberated him into a new kind of lucid, scholarly writing. He used it to try and search out 'a definition of poetry' (*BL* ii. 14): a very Coleridgian quest.

For most readers at the time and since, the passages in the *Biographia* about Wordsworth have been the most stimulating parts of the book. We know that Wordsworth read them and took them to heart; time after time, in later editions of his poetry, he would alter and adjust lines and passages which Coleridge had singled out. He also felt betrayed; he told Crabb Robinson that he found the praise of his work 'extravagant and the censure inconsiderate', while their mutual friend Lamb felt 'sure Mr. Wordsworth will never speak to Mr. Coleridge again'. He did, of course, but Robinson noted how 'cold and scornful' Wordsworth was when he met Coleridge at Christmas 1817 (*CL* IV. 757).

Fancy and Imagination

Biographia Literaria, however, also became famous for its discussion of one of Coleridge's great distinctions, that which separates 'Fancy' from 'Imagination'. The discussion was probably provoked because Wordsworth had employed both terms in his 1815 Preface, which had stated that among the powers 'requisite for the production of poetry' are 'Imagination and Fancy, – to modify, to create, and to associate' (*PW* III. 26). Wordsworth had also used the words as section titles in his poems: 'Where there is more imagination than fancy in a poem, it is placed under the head of imagination, and *vice versâ*' (*PW* III. 29). His explanations were not clear, but in the course of them he had cited Coleridge: 'Fancy has already been characterised as the power of evoking and combining, or, as my friend Mr. Coleridge has styled it, "the aggregative and associative power".' Wordsworth had, however, then commented: 'my objection is only that the definition is too general'.[9]

Such an 'objection' would have been a red rag to Coleridge, who proceeded in the *Biographia* to construct complex explanations which were yet another way of distinguishing his ways of thinking about poetry from those of his old friend. He announced that he would be doing this in chapter IV, and the original plan seems to have been for the book to proceed directly to the subject, but he interpolated a major philosophical excursus. Towards the end of what is now chapter XII, he started to make good his promise, but ominously did so by remarking that he found he differed more from Wordsworth than he had originally thought, and that Wordsworth had seriously misunderstood him.

At last, in chapter XIII, he apparently gets to work '*On the imagination, or esemplastic*[10] *power*', only to get caught up in a great string of preliminary philosophical considerations before being interrupted by a 'letter from a friend' (Coleridge himself, naturally) advising him to cut such a discussion short. Accordingly, in exactly 202 words, he at last says what he means:

> The IMAGINATION then I consider either as primary, or secondary. The primary IMAGINATION I hold to be the living Power and prime Agent of all human Perception, and as a repetition in the finite mind of the eternal act of creation in the infinite I AM. The secondary I consider as

an echo of the former, co-existing with the conscious will, yet still as identical with the primary in the *kind* of its agency, and differing only in *degree*, and in the *mode* of its operation. It dissolves, diffuses, dissipates, in order to re-create; or where this process is rendered impossible, yet still at all events it struggles to idealize and to unify. It is essentially *vital*, even as all objects (*as* objects) are essentially fixed and dead.

FANCY, on the contrary, has no other counters to play with, but fixities and definites. The Fancy is indeed no other than a mode of Memory emancipated from the order of time and space; and blended with, and modified by that empirical phenomenon of the will, which we express by the word CHOICE. But equally with the ordinary memory it must receive all its materials ready made from the law of association.

(BL I. 304–5)

Coleridge thus roundly demolishes Wordsworth's distinctions, even if his own are not altogether intelligible. What he offers, for the 'secondary' imagination of the poet, seems to be the idea that the poet (echoing the imaginative human being, who in turn reflects the divine creator), faced by experience, either recreates it or attempts 'to idealize and to unify' it. Coleridge's stress on this as 'vital' behaviour seems a way of insisting that it is largely unconscious. The poet's 'Fancy' appears to become a matter of consciously choosing and deploying literary devices (such as simile or metaphor) to comment on and illuminate experience. It is the poet's 'Imagination' which performs the initial struggle of translating experience into poetry.

It hardly matters whether Coleridge has said anything of lasting value, though the way he makes human creativity a reflection of divine creativity is characteristic. Thereafter he feels free to distinguish the words at will: 'GOOD SENSE is the BODY of poetic genius, FANCY its DRAPERY, MOTION its LIFE, and IMAGINATION the SOUL that is every where and in each' (*BL* II. 18; see too II. 127, 151). Towards the end of his final chapter on Wordsworth's poetry, he awards him praise above all for Imagination:

Last, and pre-eminently, I challenge [i.e. claim] for this poet the gift of IMAGINATION in the highest and strictest sense of the word. In the play of *Fancy*, Wordsworth, to my feelings, is not always graceful, and sometimes *recondite*. The *likeness* is occasionally too strange, or demands too peculiar a point of view, or is such as appears the creature of predetermined research, rather than spontaneous presentation. Indeed his fancy seldom displays itself, as mere and unmodified fancy. But in imaginative power, he stands nearest of all modern writers to Shakespear and Milton; and yet in a kind perfectly unborrowed and his own. (*BL* II. 151)

The praise is, as Wordsworth complained, extravagant and vague, but the criticisms of his actual writing as 'not always graceful, and sometimes *recondite*' are unremitting.

The publication and problems of the *Biographia*

The writing and production of the *Biographia* were in trouble before Coleridge had even dictated a word. Desperate for money early in 1815, he had obtained advances totalling over £100 from friends in Bristol; he had promised to reimburse them by selling a volume of his poems. This pledge committed him to supplying the poems to another friend and supporter, the Bristol printer and publisher John Mathew Gutch, leaving Gutch to arrange the printing while he himself found a publisher. He had then decided (following Wordsworth's publication of his two-volume *Poems*) to add a preface to his own poems.

The whole business dragged on for months; the preface to the poems not only grew far longer than the poems but also took a new direction when Coleridge decided to embark on a long philosophical addition. At first, two volumes were deemed necessary, one for the preface and one for the poems. Someone in Bristol, however, miscalculated the length of Coleridge's prose contribution and decided that it would need two volumes, not one. After the first volume had been printed, however, it became clear that there was after all far too little prose left for the second volume. Coleridge had to write and dispatch a good deal of extra copy. Parcels of manuscript were being sent by Coleridge or Morgan to Bristol for printing; instructions about additions and changes were constantly communicated by letter; proof sheets were sent to Coleridge, not all of which he returned on time. Delay after delay resulted. Type was expensively kept standing at the printers, no money was earned by anyone. The sheets were being printed in Bristol but published in London; the publisher complained that so many sheets were damaged in transit that he could not make up the required number of finished books, while one of the original supporters of the project, a Mr Le Breton, refused to allow a parcel of sheets to be posted to London before he got back from Coleridge the £14 he had volunteered. The three volumes (the poems as *Sibylline Leaves*, with their own short Preface) did not finally appear until July 1817 – Coleridge would call them 'delay'd two years' (*CL* iv. 758) – and it was only then that the Bristol benefactors recovered their money.

The first readers of the *Biographia* found an even more varied book than now appears in many reprints. Desperate for materials to fill up the gap in the second volume left by the miscalculation of its length, Coleridge seems first to have extended chapter XXII, partly by quoting a great deal more of Wordsworth's poetry. He then dug out the letters from Germany he had originally knocked into shape as 'Satyrane's Letters' for *The Friend* in 1809 and inserted them after chapter XXII; he also included (as chapter XXIII) a condensed version of a long critique of Maturin's play *Bertram* that he had recently dictated to Morgan for the *Courier* and so had to hand when materials for the *Biographia* were most badly needed. Furthermore, he added a chapter XXIV written in reply to some of the critics of his recent published work. These chapters are sometimes omitted from reprints of *Biographia*, but they originally made for an even odder book and would have given its first readers an even greater impression of disorganisation.

The nature of the *Biographia*

As ever, it was one of Coleridge's ideals to make his own intellectual activity and struggle the main subject of his discourse; his principal interest was in the very process of thinking and making. (This incidentally makes all the odder his poetic ideal of the 'organic Whole': the idea that, in the great poem, no word could be changed, no word's position altered – *BL* I. 23, 234.) The *Biographia* has been defended as offering 'an organised unity' and even 'a series of interlocking unities',[11] but it provides most of its readers with a fascinating but maddening mixture of autobiography, self-defence, unfulfilled promises, anecdote, literary criticism, psychology, intellectual history, philosophy and religion. Most innocent readers will find such things coming at them with very little sense of link or connection; at times confusedly, at other times lucidly. One chapter heading runs: '*A Chapter of requests and premonitions concerning the perusal or omission of the chapter that follows*', which will leave most readers open-mouthed, while they will probably skip entirely prose as dense as this:

> This principium commune essendi et cognoscendi, as subsisting in a WILL, or primary ACT of self-duplication, is the mediate or indirect principle of every science; but it is the immediate and direct principle of the ultimate science alone, i.e. of transcendental philosophy alone. For it must be remembered, that all these Theses refer solely to one of the two Polar Sciences, namely, to that which commences with and rigidly confines itself within the subjective, leaving the objective (as far as it is exclusively objective) to natural philosophy, which is its opposite pole.   (*BL* I. 281–2)

The fact that Coleridge felt it necessary to write to his printer and supporter Gutch defending the 'philosophical Part' as 'with the exception of four or five Pages of which due warning is given, the most *entertaining* to the general Reader' (*CL* iv. 586) suggests how uncertain he must really have been about it. An 1817 reviewer singled out that very passage as baffling, and nothing has occurred over the last 200 years to make it easier.

The great Coleridge scholar Kathleen Coburn was right to suggest that a notebook entry containing a fragment from Milton would have made a good epigraph for the *Biographia*: '"Instead of outward actions to bring [our] inmost Thoughts into Front" Milt. Apol. –' (*CN* i. 700). The 'outward actions' of the book are as strange, confusing and at times mysterious as could be imagined. The 'inmost thoughts' are utterly compelling. Coleridge left a book that, in many ways more like a miscellany, contains material enough for a dozen books. He also never allows us to forget just what a writer he is. He describes a Birmingham tallow chandler with 'thin gunpowder eye brows, that looked like a scorched *after-math* from a last week's shaving'; he suggests that the only state of mind to which the philosophy of David Hartley is truly appropriate is 'that of complete light-headedness' (*BL* i. 180, 112). The anecdotes are among his most cheerful; his Wordsworth criticism is still well worth reading.

Another kind of autobiography

One of the most striking things about the *Biographia*, however, was that after having apparently established its subjects – Coleridge's own life, the nature of poetry and the work of Wordsworth – the book then ensures that, for the run of chapters V through IX, and then for most of XII–XIII, such things receive barely a mention. Coleridge apparently wishes to demonstrate how the words 'Fancy' and 'Imagination' really should be used, and embarks on a very different kind of autobiography. He constructs a kind of intellectual (and spiritual) history of how someone like himself had come into existence, which is another way for him to show the sources of his real authority and expertise; sources that have nothing to do with Wordsworth.

Accordingly, chapters V–IX and XII–XIII of the *Biographia* offer a kind of grand intellectual history. With the avowed objective of explaining 'Fancy' and 'Imagination', associationism, idealism and materialism are summed up (along with Hobbes, Descartes, Hartley and Bishop Berkeley) and dismissed; Kant, Schelling and the German philosopher Fichte are explored and apparently developed – thus allowing Coleridge to demonstrate just how much he knew about modern philosophy and where it was going (or ought to go).

The seriousness of these chapters, however, has been undermined by the way they have been demonstrated to depend upon an unacknowledged series of borrowings from German philosophers. Far from being an account of an individual intellectual history, the chapters are a tissue of quotation and paraphrase of other writers.

Intellectual property and the *Biographia*

De Quincey wrote after Coleridge's death accusing him of plagiarism,[12] and many have followed up the charge. Coleridge's notebooks usefully demonstrate how easily his borrowings might end up misattributed. In London in March 1804, for example, he read and was delighted by Thomas Cartwright's *Comedies, Tragi-Comedies, With Other Poems* of 1651. He copied extracts into his notebooks. At times he made a note about the author, e.g. 'Love's Convert/ by Cartwright', but many extracts bear no trace of their origin, any more than do lines cited from Charles Cotton in 1809 or quotations from Fulke Greville in 1810 (*CN* II. 1943, III. 3654, 3709–12). As a result, many of the quoted lines have every appearance of being poetry of Coleridge's own, and passages of Cartwright and Greville were printed as Coleridge's in *Literary Remains*, *Anima Poetae* and again in his *Poetical Works* in 1912. The discovery of their real authors quite unfairly appeared to extend the range of Coleridge's plagiarisms.

He regularly rephrased what he borrowed. Sir William Davenant had described 'a summer passage on a crooked River, where going about, and turning back is as delightful as the delayes of parting lovers'. Coleridge wrote into his notebook: 'A summer Sailing on a still peninsulating River, and sweet as the delays of parting Lovers' (*CN* III. 3771), without acknowledging Davenant. Was he remembering and relishing his reading or was he plagiarising it?

In other cases he transformed what he took. A remark in a sermon by Robert South (a successful politician must 'abhor gratitude, as a worse kind of witchcraft, which only serves to conjure up the pale, meager ghosts') became quite new in Coleridge's version: 'Gratitude/worse than Witchcraft – conjures up the pale, meager ghosts of dead, forgotten kindnesses, to haunt & trouble him – '; while a dull sentence in South – 'The thread that nature spins, is seldom broken off by any thing but death' – was magically renewed in Coleridge's note: 'And death alone breaks off the thread, that Nature spins' (*CN* I. 323, III. 4004). He also had a marvellous memory. A line he had read in 1796 in Thomas Sackville, 'Wishing for death, and yet she could not die' (*CN* I. 98 n.), but did not include in his notebook, bubbled up in 'The Ancient Mariner' a couple of years later, when he wrote 'And yet I could not die' (*CPI* I. 392).

The unacknowledged use of material in the *Biographia*, so often commented on by hostile and friendly critics alike, is, however, a still odder business. Coleridge quoted and translated freely, mostly without acknowledgement. A paragraph translated from Lessing appeared, for example, without inverted commas in chapter XXI (*BL* ii. 109 and n. 2), while chapters V–IX could simply not have been written without passages which either translated, para-phrased or amplified Schelling's words. The especially baffling passage I quoted above was, for example, almost entirely paraphrase and translation of Schelling (*BL* i. 281–3 nn.).

The usual discussion centres on whether Coleridge should be condemned for plagiarism, as we would condemn a contemporary writer, or be excused because he was writing as a philosophical ironist, because he was introducing an element of 'psycho-drama' into his work, or because, after all, he always gave to others more than he stole, which was De Quincey's conclusion in 1834.[13] In his letters and talk he had regularly passed on quantities of original ideas and material to others, though he had at times resented how many people seemed to have taken the credit for what he had given them.

Discussion, however, rather than mediating between condemnation and excuses, needs to understand what Coleridge was doing. He knew how a writer like himself, constantly drawing upon the past, with his memory and his notebooks steeped in what he had read, might be seen as – might well *be* – a plagiarist. When, however, he included in his notebook a little aphorism about plagiarists ('Plagiarists *suspicious* of being pilfer'd – as pick-pockets are observed commonly to walk with their hands in their breeches-pockets' – *CN* i. 224) it was apparently without the least consciousness that he might be saying something about himself.

He had, however, believed all his life that learning of various kinds, and the writing of others, was (or ought to be) at his fingertips. He hardly ever bothered about the authorship of what he read or noted or quoted. He had singled it out as part of his resources; and if it helped illuminate his point of view, then it was his to use. He might not always have written enough, but at least he had done the reading; he also found it natural to identify himself with a writer with whom he agreed, so that 'his thoughts become my thoughts' (*CM* vi. 305). Not for nothing was he a staunch believer in the importance of imitation in love and learning: 'we unconsciously imitate those whom we love' (*CN* i. 191 n.).

He frequently insisted, too, that he had anticipated in intellectual discovery those whom he had read. He wrote confidently how 'In Schelling's "Natur-Philosophie," and the "System des transcendentalen Idealismus," I first found a genial coincidence with much that I had toiled out for myself, and a powerful assistance in what I had yet to do.' He claimed that all his 'main and fundamental ideas . . . were born and matured in my mind before I had ever seen a single page of the German Philosopher' (*BL* I. 160). Such claims do not stand up, in spite of some efforts over the years to show how they might.[14] But Coleridge's belief that he *had* worked out the ideas for himself doubtless assisted him in recycling what he chose to believe was no more than coincidental with his own work.

He was, furthermore, prepared to ignore a great deal that Kant and Schelling had actually argued, for the sake of promoting 'a philosophy that serves a religion'.[15] Over and over again in the *Biographia* he imposes religious conclusions on to arguments which have nothing to do with religion. In chapter VIII, for example, having without acknowledgement quoted and paraphrased Schelling throughout a long paragraph, he suddenly introduces a quotation from Cowley apparently summing up the argument: 'And like a God by spiritual art, / Be all in all, and all in every part' (*BL* I. 134). But Schelling had said nothing about God.

Again, in chapter XII of the *Biographia*, he constructs ten Theses from various statements by Schelling, and Thesis VI includes Schelling's basic statement of self-awareness, 'I am because I am' ('sum quia sum' in Latin). Coleridge however adds 'But if . . . he be again asked how he, the individual person, came to be, then . . . he might reply, sum quia deus est [I am because God is]' (*BL* I. 274). Schelling had explicitly set aside this position as untenable in theoretical philosophy; like Kant in his first *Critique*, Schelling had argued that philosophy cannot state that God is 'the ground of our *knowledge*' (*BL* I. 274 n. 2). Coleridge, un-philosophically but instinctively, assumes it; he had a 'tendency to personalise the Absolute, and so turn a logical function into a character from Divinity'.[16] He had always been 'a Christian thinker'; in the 1820s he would assert that the Trinity was 'the primary Idea, out of which all other Ideas are evolved'.[17] In the *Biographia* we can observe exactly how his commitment to Christianity overcomes his philosophical judgement.

Another example comes in Thesis X. Coleridge has been translating and paraphrasing Schelling to assert that 'the true system of natural philosophy places the sole reality of things in an ABSOLUTE'; he then adds 'In this sense the position of Malbranche, that we see all things in God, is a strict philosophical truth' (*BL* I. 285). Once again, the Christian God is substituted for what Schelling had actually been discussing: the 'idealistic ABSOLUTE' which is the consciousness of one's own consciousness ('*all* Consciousness is necessarily conditioned by Self-consciousness').[18]

In such ways, Coleridge's argument is 'not so much derived from German sources as it is belligerent to them'.[19] He had both the confidence and the anxiety of the philosopher who was also a religious thinker. His work, 'long-continued and arduous theological Reading & Reflection' (*CL* iv. 764), had been carried out a very long way, literally, from other scholars. By 1815 he knew that, in the eyes of the world, he had been wasting his time and talents for years; his friends desired to see him 'address the whole powers of his soul to some great work in prose or verse, of which the effect would be permanent', not to events like his lectures, 'personal and transitory' (*LW* ii. 1. 83). The *Biographia* was his first original prose book and the first completely new book he had brought out since 1796. Like *The Friend*, it offered him an opportunity to do something with the material he had been studying for years. He badly needed to show what he was capable of; he also wanted to demonstrate that he was a philosopher and Wordsworth was not.

It has been suggested that he plagiarised Schelling and others because of the self-doubt which stemmed from his opium addiction.[20] I suspect the opposite to have been the case. He was a man who 'could not bear to live without admiration & notoriety' (*OM* cxlviii–cxlix); with Morgan's help he was getting his life back on an even keel, and he grasped his opportunity to deploy material of which very few of his contemporaries were aware (hardly anyone in England was as well read in German philosophy as he). Accordingly he quoted it, borrowed from it, plagiarised it, but in some sense made it his own while doing so – by altering its conclusions so that it said what he wanted it to say.

This was no ordinary kind of plagiarism. Not only did Coleridge not share modern attitudes towards the acknowledgement of sources, but he ensured that what he took from others conformed to the intellectual positions he had adopted. He wanted support from his sources, but also ensured that he found it; they were obliged to fall into line with the direction in which he took them.

Onwards from the *Biographia*

That Coleridge might be seen sailing confidently forward on a great surge of coherent thinking, theory and explanation was very important to him. He even sent a copy of the *Biographia*, along with an enormously long letter, to the Prime Minister, Lord Liverpool. It had been Liverpool's administration which, six months earlier, had been responsible for the suspension of habeas corpus (the Prince Regent's coach had been attacked on its way to the state opening of Parliament, and those supporting parliamentary reform had been blamed). The government had quickly got on to the statute book the so-called Gagging Acts, banning meetings of more than fifty people and cracking down on those accused of 'seditious libel'. In 1795, Coleridge had written brilliantly against two very similar Gagging Acts. In 1817 he wrote a humble letter to the Prime Minister. His situation in 1817 was very different; he was desperate for money, he needed support. The letter was to no avail. Liverpool annotated the massive screed Coleridge sent him with a brief objective summary and the terribly understandable comment: 'at least I believe this is Mr. Coleridge's meaning, but I cannot well understand him' (*CL* iv. 757).

Behind everything that Coleridge argued for was the implicit (and at times explicit) promise that what he was saying in the *Biographia* would be surpassed in his next book. For he announced that he would shortly be publishing a book that would sum up, 'at large and systematically', the new and superior (because explicitly religious) version of European philosophy which he had hinted at in *Biographia Literaria*. The forthcoming book (*Logosophia*: i.e., the wisdom of the Logos, the divine Word) would be 'a work, which I have been many years preparing, on the PRODUCTIVE LOGOS human and divine' (*BL* i. 136).

Coleridge would have been aware that his 'philosophy' in *Biographia Literaria* had attempted to bolt on to existing Idealistic philosophy elements of the Christian revelation. All he could do was hope that his next publication would be more comprehensive and systematic, and state that it would be advertised at the end of the *Biographia* (*BL* i. 263). In fact there is no reference to it there, nor indeed anywhere else. It was the book he always wanted to write but could not. The two philosophical volumes today generally called Coleridge's *Logic* and his *Opus Maximum*, dictated in the 1820s, no longer had the title *Logosophia* – and neither would be finished, either, under any title.

We have no idea whether Coleridge believed that, in writing and publishing the *Biographia*, he had at last established himself. It seems doubtful. He was still insisting that his major life-work, philosophical and religious, lay ahead of him; he believed that only with the *Logosophia* would he manage to ground his reputation (*CL* iv. 589). The *Biographia* remains a kind of beached whale; a book to wander around in and enjoy, to stop and marvel at, to peer into and refer to and learn from, but not to treat as if it were a self-consistent work of criticism, or of philosophy, or indeed of anything else recognised as a coherent discipline.

Chapter 7

Later works and contexts: 1815–1834

Coleridge's crisis in his early forties was brought to an end by his placing himself in the hands of people (first the Morgans, then the Gillmans) who were prepared to care for him. With their encouragement and help he was able to find a kind of equilibrium in his opium use between quantities that provoked withdrawal symptoms and quantities that made it nearly impossible for him to function.

As late as 1814, while aware that opium was the cause of his problems, Coleridge had only been able to understand his illness as that of an 'utter impotence of the *Volition*'; it felt as if his will had been afflicted by a kind of madness (*CL* ii. 953). In 1820, however, he would describe how 'my *Body* had contracted a habit & a necessity', which was a clear step forward in locating the problem not within the domain of will-power but within the body itself. He still nevertheless felt horribly responsible for his 'defect of fortitude' and 'cowardice of pain' (*CL* v. 80, *CN* ii. 2495) in not being able to withstand the agonies of withdrawal: 'loathes while he takes, yet still takes, goaded on by pain, and more than pain, and by the dread of both' (*CM* v. 419). De Quincey's *Confessions of an English Opium Eater* of 1821, in which the author boasted of having triumphed over *his* opium habit, would, however, have confirmed to Coleridge's acquaintances that (as they suspected) he was simply not trying hard enough. It seemed natural to accuse a man of hypocrisy who argued for religion and morality while living apart from his wife and indulging in opium;

113

Coleridge's nephew John felt a 'painful wonder' when observing how 'a man who can think and speak as he does... should have acted and still act as he has done and does' (*TT* I. 16). But by moving in with the Morgans and then the Gillmans, Coleridge had given himself at least a chance of leading a less incoherent life.

The thirty-four year-old surgeon James Gillman had no idea of inviting Coleridge into his family home in Highgate until April 1816, when – 'stunn'd' like the wedding-guest in 'The Ancient Mariner' by Coleridge's conversation – 'I felt indeed almost spell-bound, without the desire of release.'[1] Coleridge, ten years older, accepted Gillman's offer to be his medical adviser and also (in effect) his asylum keeper, himself the 'dangerous Lunatic' (*CN* IV. 4511). In so doing, he had to accept the kinds of restrictions which he knew would conflict with his raging bodily demand for opium; but Gillman would give him a home and regulate his dose, not attempt to reform him.

Coleridge thus committed himself to a life of retirement, in which his faith became a constantly re-invented source of security for him, as he stabilised himself after the chaos and desperation of his middle years. But it could not render his daily existence normal; for that he needed Gillman. Supported by his friendship with Morgan, he had managed to dictate his *Biographia Literaria*, and now, living with the Gillmans, he dictated his first explicitly religious publications, the two *Lay Sermons* (published 1816–17). He also worked with Gillman on producing the essay posthumously published as his *Theory of Life* (1848), worked hard on a book on logic (published posthumously), wrote and published *Aids to Reflection* in 1825 and, in 1829, brought out *On the Constitution of the Church and State*.

Not everything went smoothly. The dictated publications were frequently peculiar in their organisation and their use of extended footnotes and additional appendices. Furthermore, Coleridge continued to obtain extra doses of opium in spite of Gillman, and he abandoned the Gillman household at least once. But he needed the family too much to hold out for long, and allowed himself to be fetched 'home'. First Moreton House and, from November 1823, the attic room at The Grove were his home now, just as his Thursday evenings in the drawing-room below became his social world. He was starting to be visited by people; the young poet John Keats was introduced to him as he walked over Highgate Hill one Sunday afternoon in 1819; the Scottish writer Thomas Carlyle and the youthful writer and journalist Harriet Martineau both came, while in 1833, the young American essayist Ralph Waldo Emerson visited. Coleridge accepted the role they gave him as one of the great sages of the day.

Religion

By 1801 Coleridge had been increasingly doubtful of his Unitarianism, noting that the next step for the Unitarian was to 'go either to the Trinity or to Pantheism'; in August 1805 he proclaimed the doctrine of the Trinity a 'Truth' (*CN* ii. 2640). By 1806, he was staunchly Church of England. His vague plans for what he had once called 'my curious Metaphysical work' (*CL* ii. 776) – in 1796–7 he had dubbed it a work 'for and against Natural and revealed Religion' (*CL* i. 209) – became focused during the first decade of the nineteenth century on a synthesis of the arguments in favour of Christianity which had been propagated over the centuries. This would be 'my *System* of Thought on God, Nature, and Man – namely, that which aims to prove, that Christianity is true in Reason' (*CN* v. 6737). Where he had once thought that the best propaganda for Christianity was 'the weak Argument that do yet persuade so many to believe – i.e. it fits the human heart' (*CN* i. 1123), he now believed he could show how the human mind engaged with reason and truths, and thus conceived of God. He would argue that the sciences of which he was so aware, as well as German philosophy, could be made consistent with 'fundamental Christian principles about God, nature and man'.[2] His study of the *Logos* (the Greek word often used as the particular Christian term for God and Christ) revealed it to him as the rational principle in the universe, and Coleridge always insisted on the truths of reason; but it was also 'the Word' revealed at the start of St John's gospel ('In the beginning was the Word'). And for Coleridge *language* was supreme in both religious and human experience.

Because Coleridge was possessed of an amazingly subtle and complex mind, his sense of religion was inevitably complex and dense; only very late in life would he define the 'main points' of his faith as 'a personal God, a surviving principle of Life, & that I need & that I have a Redeemer' (*CL* vi. 577) – and even in that formulation, the 'surviving principle of Life' would cover almost anything. He was more honest in his 1824 confession that, after a life such as his, he felt strongly 'the want, the necessity, of religious support' (*SWF* ii. 1117). In his secure establishment from 1816 onwards, he would demonstrate a newly polemical religious orthodoxy. He continued his deep thinking for the old 'Logosophia' project, the one he had previously always failed to undertake; but, confident that he was again able to dictate and publish, he could also address himself to the general educated public in more practical ways. He became extremely influential as a thinker on spiritual matters in the first half of the nineteenth century; in 1826, the University of Vermont would have its curriculum changed by its president to one based on 'Coleridgian transcendental lines'.[3]

Lay Sermons

Coleridge's first lay sermon was entitled *The Statesman's Manual, or The Bible the Best Guide to Political Skill and Foresight*, and appeared in December 1816, addressed to 'the higher classes of society', 'more particularly to the learned' (*LS* xxxi). A second sermon appeared in the spring of 1817; a planned-for third never materialised. Coleridge was inventing a genre all his own: topical rhetoric about matters of the day, starting with a text from the Bible and making constant reference to religion and the scriptures. Reflections and quotations are inserted as a kind of luminous commentary (or 'Best Guide'); Christianity is presented as '*grounded* on *facts*' (*LS* 55). His political journalism about contemporary issues had been rather similar, but with the single exception of his campaign in newspapers between 1816 and 1818 against child labour in factories, with its glinting, savage irony (*EHT* ii. 484–9, iii. 145–6, 155–8), he now preferred the space which an individual publication allowed. Such a pamphlet offered him the opportunity for innumerable footnotes, extra passages, appendices, qualifications and further reflections which a newspaper editor would certainly have expunged and which at times almost submerge the main text.

The religious attitudes Coleridge adopted were not something that most newspapers would have enjoyed, either. He did not hesitate to denounce Unitarians and condemn conventional Protestant groups for being utterly unreflecting about their religion (he complained that they think it 'so very easy' – *LS* 6, 194). He also ridiculed the evangelistic movement for its naivety, called the Roman Catholic Church 'the Church of Superstition' (*LS* 6) and made snide remarks about the extravagant commercial wealth generated by individual Quakers. Examples of his unorthodox stance were his attitude towards the doctrine of the redemption (the idea 'of a vicarious Satisfaction' – God being satisfied by Christ's crucifixion – 'I reject not without some horror' – *CL* iii. 128), and his remarkable openness towards the idea of Transubstantiation, as opposed to the symbolic qualities of the Communion sacrament invested in Anglican doctrine (*CN* iii. 3848 n.). Hazlitt would indeed accuse him of 'potential infidelity', but Coleridge positively enjoyed being out of step with his contemporaries. In 1823 he would write down – though leave unfinished – the deeply subversive story

of Oran & St Columba – whose first Building on Iona fell down by
machination of some evil Spirit – A human offering being required, S^t
Oran offered himself, & was buried alive – but at the end of 3 Days S^t
Columba wishing to have another look of his old Companion had the
earth removed when up started Oran all alive & kicking – & began by
informing them that all, they had been taught to believe of Hell &c. was
a humbug – St Columba alarmed set to work himself & disciples in
shovelling back the earth upon the Blab and in a few minutes put an
end to his . . .   (*CN* iv. 5031 and n.)

It was Charles Lamb who commented enigmatically, when asked why his
old friend was now so terribly religious, 'Ah, there is a g-g-great deal of fun
in Coleridge!'[4] In religion and politics, Coleridge positioned himself as the
outsider who was really able to understand what is going on, being both
shrewd and unusual, *and* equipped with principles 'as taught in the Bible'
(*LS* 17).

The second sermon, however, is most interesting today as an illumination
of Coleridge's very personal variety of conservatism; by no means the simple
reactionary politics of which he was accused by people like Hazlitt, but a
historically rooted conservatism in which he regularly aligns himself with
radical positions (he makes much, for example, of Milton). At times he violently
attacks the attitudes of radicals like William Cobbett; at other times he equally
enthusiastically agrees with them, as when he joins in the condemnation of
paper money and the national debt (*LS* 212). Time and again his writing grows
powerful when he describes actual people:

> Persons are not *Things* . . . Alas! I have more than once seen a group of
> children in Dorsetshire, during the heat of the dog-days, each with its
> little shoulders up to its ears, and its chest pinched inward, the very
> habit and *fixtures*, as it were, that had been impressed on their frames by
> the former ill-fed, ill-clothed, and unfuelled winters.   (*LS* 206–7)

Above all he enjoys casting himself in the role of a Jeremiah for his society, one
denouncing the 'Spirit of Barter', 'the commercial spirit' and the 'sorcery of
wealth' (*LS* 195, 199); he stands up for the rights and needs of the agricultural
labourer and refuses to accept 'the poor' as a social category at all. In February
1832 he would attack the very 'Custom of addressing *"The Poor"*' as 'One of the
ominous characteristics of this reforming Age' and marking 'a most deplorable
State of Society' (*CN* v. 6655).

Faustus

During these early Highgate years, Coleridge veered between cheerfulness and depression; he drafted the occasional poem, wrote constantly in his notebooks, studied the Bible and talked at enormous length whenever he could. It has been claimed that he was also responsible for an anonymous, partial, verse translation of Goethe's *Faust*, published in 1821 to accompany twenty-six engravings; the attribution has, however, been fiercely contested.[5] Coleridge certainly negotiated in the spring of 1820 with the publisher who wanted to issue such a work, but late in life declared 'I never put pen to paper as translator of Faust' (*TT* I. 343).

There were, however, good reasons why he would have wanted to disclaim responsibility for the translation of a work regarded in some quarters as anti-Christian; and if he had dictated such a translation (as he almost certainly would have done), then he might have been telling the truth about never putting pen to paper. Following the collapse in 1819 of Rest Fenner, the publisher of *Biographia Literaria*, *Sibylline Leaves*, his *Lay Sermons* and a revised reprint of *The Friend*, he was in need of any money he could earn; the translation, moreover, borrows from work done in 1820 by a young man called John Anster, of whom Coleridge saw a good deal during the months when he would been working on such a project.

The translation is, however, not brilliant and contains some significant differences from the German original. It reproduces one of the most touching of Gretchen's songs ('Meine Ruh' ist hin / Mein Herz ist schwer; / Ich finde sie nimmer / Und nimmermehr') as

> My peace of mind's ruined;
> My bosom is sore,
> I ne'er meet him now,
> I shall ne'er meet him more.[6]

The translation, advertised as being done by 'A Gentleman of Literary Eminence', employs a number of convenient changes (in that verse, Gretchen should not be talking about 'him' – Faust – at all, only about her inner peace), but we know that Coleridge believed that verse translation should be as free as necessary (*CL* VI. 1052–3). My suspicion is that he may have done the translation as hack work, but it does him little credit. Such a work should certainly not be celebrated as one of his major achievements.

Aids to Reflection

The massive title of Coleridge's second religious publication (*Aids to Reflection in the Formation of a Manly Character on the Several Grounds of Prudence, Morality, and Religion: Illustrated by Select Passages from our Elder Divines, especially from Archbishop Leighton*) demonstrates not only the book's complex origins but its considerable ambitions. It began as selected passages from a commentary on the first epistle of Peter by Robert Leighton, a seventeenth-century divine who became Archbishop of Glasgow. Coleridge interjected his own aphorisms, suggestions and further quotations so that eventually the material became so extensive that he decided to publish commentary, quotations and aphorisms all together.

However, not every edition shows which parts of the book Coleridge wrote. The 1831 second edition removed many of the notes indicating which were Leighton's words and which were Coleridge's. Leighton's remark 'He never truly believed, who was not made first sensible and convinced of unbelief' (*CM* III. 572, *AR* 107) is for example immediately followed by Coleridge's own comment: 'Never be afraid to doubt, if only you have the disposition to believe, and doubt in order that you may end in believing the Truth.' Readers in 1825 perhaps assumed that both aphorisms were Leighton's; later readers probably imagined both were Coleridge's. Coleridge did however add ('in my own name and from my own conviction') the following:

> APHORISM XXV
> He, who begins by loving Christianity better than Truth, will proceed by loving his own Sect or Church better than Christianity, and end in loving himself better than all.   (*AR* 107: see too *CN* IV. 5026)

It is a comment aimed partly at his own Unitarianism and at his escape from it, but it is directed primarily at religious enthusiasm everywhere; Coleridge found Methodism, for example, peculiarly selfish in its insistence that Christ 'died for *my* Sins, even *mine*, and saved *me*' (*CN* III. 3901).

It has been claimed that Coleridge's *Aids to Reflection* sets out 'to hand on as directly as possible the fruits of his own spiritual experience', experience which 'could not be separated from his previous intellectual and psychical development' (*AR* xii). Most modern readers will find the book rather lacking in accounts of Coleridge's 'intellectual and psychical development', and unless they especially enjoy the religious exposition are likely to find it disappointing. It is, however, a book that shows how impressive Coleridge must have been as a preacher. In spite of Charles Lamb's witty response to Coleridge's question

'Have you ever heard me preach, Charles?' – 'N-n-never heard you d-d-do anything else, C-c-coleridge' (*LS* xxv) – preaching was only *one* of Coleridge's modes, but *Aids to Reflection* displays him in full flow:

> Behold the shadow of approaching Humanity, the Sun rising from behind, in the kindling Morn of Creation! Thus all lower Natures find their highest Good in semblances and seekings of that which is higher and better. All things strive to ascend, and ascend in their striving. And shall man alone stoop? Shall his pursuits and desires, the *reflections* of his inward life, be like the reflected Image of a Tree on the edge of a Pool, that grows downward . . . ? No! it must be a higher good to make you happy. While you labor for any thing below your proper Humanity, you seek a happy Life in the region of Death.   (*AR* 118–19)

The final phrase is a quotation from St Augustine's *Confessions*, though the heaped-up rhetorical questions find a more natural parallel in the preachifying of Mr Chadband in Dickens's *Bleak House* (1853).[7] Such passages, however, became famous; Emerson would include 'All things strive to ascend & ascend in their striving' in a notebook (*AR* cxxvi).

Aids to Reflection was ultimately valuable in that it made Coleridge's name as a religious thinker, especially in America. The aphoristic style in which much of the book is couched, and into which Coleridge recast it during writing and proof-editing (*AR* lxv), means that, for some of the time at least, late Coleridge reads easily, though the footnotes are likely to trip up all but the very committed reader.

More suggestive still, as John Beer has pointed out (*AR* lxxxviii–xcvi), is Coleridge's use of the word 'Reflection'. He had always used the word in its usual senses, for example remembering the Maltese sea as 'the substantial Image and fixed real Reflection of the Sky' (*CN* II. 3159), and referring to the end of 'The Statesman's Manual' as 'a maniple or handful of loose flowers, a string of Hints and Material for Reflection' (*LS* 114 n. 2). Yet even those quotations suggest something further. The mind that studiously reflects *on* something (Coleridge called this activity 'natural consciousness' – *BL* I. 154) also appears, in the process, to be *reflecting* something outside it that is still more real. The sea does not just mirror the sky but also, as 'the substantial Image' of it, allows insight into the real nature of the sky. Just so, the reflecting mind does not just ponder things outside itself, nor simply bounce back a mirror image; it acts as a focus for what lies outside it and by doing so takes upon itself something of the nature of what it reflects.

'Reflexion seems the first approach to, & shadow of, the divine Permanency' (*CL* II. 1197), Coleridge had suggested in 1806, when he also coined the phrase 'reflex consciousness' to describe what happens in this more complex process of reflection. Such reflection allows the individual to acquire 'knowledge . . . not received from the senses', 'the existence of which we can prove to others, only as far as we can prevail on them to *go into themselves* and make their own minds the Object of their stedfast attention' (*Friend* ii. 7 n. 1): yet another kind of reflection. This returns us to a characteristic Coleridgian comment about language, that 'The best part of human language, properly so called, is derived from reflection on the acts of the mind itself' (*BL* ii. 54); reflection in every sense.

On the Constitution of the Church and State

It was typical of Coleridge that his contribution to a pressing political question of the 1820s – what Roman Catholic emancipation would mean for the Church of England and its place in the British constitution – should have taken such a very far-reaching form. In *On the Constitution of the Church and State* he engaged in an exploration of the deep structure of the implications of the 1829 Emancipation Act, which aimed to free Roman Catholics from the civil disabilities imposed upon them (no Catholic could sit in Parliament, for example). Coleridge believed the Act had been insufficiently thought through and suspected that it was a piece of political expediency. He also insisted that the ideas involved had not been properly considered (his title continued *According to the Idea of Each*).

The book was published in December 1829 at what Coleridge called the '*choking* price' of half a guinea (*CL* vi. 825); a second edition, slightly more carefully organised and arranged, came out soon afterwards. It did not attract many reviews or original readers, but in the long run it proved to be deeply influential on men like John Henry Newman, who initiated the Oxford Movement, and F. D. Maurice, who appreciated its careful thinking about the nature of the Church of England. In particular, it used the word 'clerisy' (appropriated from the old German *die Klerisei*) to describe the scholars of a nation, 'its learned – its poets – its writers' (*TT* i. 285), who ideally make up the Church. The word would resonate for decades.

Coleridge's later prose writing is problematic for most readers because it is so complicated. The dictation to which he had become habituated encouraged him to stretch his sentence length until it became a python coiling around his meanings, parenthesis following parenthesis. Add the complexity of the writing to the fact that the subject is itself rather dense (its most recent editor recommends that one reads Henry Nelson Coleridge's Introduction to the

1839 edition before even starting Coleridge's own work — *C&S* lix) and *On the Constitution of the Church and State* is never going to attract many modern readers.

Coleridge's characteristic liveliness still, however, gets into the book. In an 'Author's Appendix' he prints a revised version of a letter he had written to his nephew three years earlier, which is a kind of brief testament of the grounds for belief. Human beings may live in one world, but experience should convince them of their adaptation for another world. Just as the eyes, ears and lungs of the unborn child demonstrate its fitness for another world, so man has 'the idea of the good, the idea of the beautiful, ideas of eternity, immortality, freedom', and these should demonstrate to him 'this other world ... yea, it is his proper home. But he is an absentee and *chooses* to live abroad' (*C&S* 176–7). The 'Author's Appendix' has almost nothing to do with the subject of the book; it has indeed been condemned as part of the book's 'disastrously ragged ending' (*C&S* lvii), but it is thoroughly entertaining. So far as the body of the book is concerned, though, while historians of the Church of England and the Irish question appreciate its attempt to set out the issues at an important historical moment, *On the Constitution of the Church and State* will remain for most readers the least compelling of Coleridge's major works.

Later life

Coleridge's friends were very conscious of what a deprived life he had been forced to lead. Charles Lamb pointed out, after Sarah Coleridge had visited Highgate together with their daughter Sara in 1822, 'Poor C. I wish had a home to receive his daughter in. But he is as a stranger or visitor in this world.'[8] Coleridge had now been without a home of his own since 1803. His life in Highgate was interrupted only by his participation in the Gillmans' family holidays, sometimes at Ramsgate (when he could afford to go: 'Poverty and I are a match made in heaven' – *CN* III. 4498), and by a rather strange expedition to the Continent he undertook at the last minute with Dorothy and William Wordsworth in the summer of 1828. He was ill rather often, but not to an extent which suppressed his fascination with the world around him. At a sea-bathing establishment at Zandvoort, he copied out a 'splendid specimen of Dutch English' proclaiming that the public 'will be saved in a most satisfying manner' (*CN* v. 5912). He also scribbled terrible denunciations of Wordsworth into his notebook:

he never reconsiders, or stops to think if one has already understood him, but each word is followed by three, four, five syn – or homoeonyms [i.e. words or names *like* words or names used to denote different things], in an exhausting train of eddies, and like this for three, four hours – albeit for the most part reasonable, but just reasonable commonplaces – no highlights, no felicities – for the innumerable dissonances which his way of thinking, of feeling, of acting created with my own, repulsed me at every moment – the very worst being his considerable anxiety over money and trifling money-matters/

(*CN* v. 5904)

It is significant that it should have been Wordsworth's language which was one of things that now so irritated Coleridge; we can imagine him bottling himself up and growing furious while Wordsworth talked, during their long coach journeys.

Talking and thinking

People who liked to talk themselves usually never had a chance if Coleridge were there; only his irritation with Wordsworth could have kept him silent in 1828. Innumerable anecdotes survive: from his Harz walking tour in 1799 when 'talk seemed to him a perennial pastime', to a man who met him in Brussels in 1828 and noted how 'He seemed to breathe in words.'[9] An acquaintance who saw him three weeks before his death observed that he still talked with 'vigour and animation', although '*speaking* at all' was difficult (*TT* I. lxxiii). He regularly celebrated his delight in his own talk, dazzling 'the bye-stander' as he would 'with colors succeeding so rapidly as to leave one vague impression that there has been a great Blaze of colours all about something' (*CN* II. 2372).

The talk for which he would become famous might also be seen as a kind of showing to others what he had read and thought. It was, quite simply, communicative, an implicit appeal for the understanding of others; as he would note in 1808, with his usual psychological acuity, his own 'social nature compels *some* Outlet' (*CN* III. 3325). One of his listeners once commented that Coleridge's talk seemed 'so full of information that it was a relief to him to part with some portion of it to others. It was like laying down part of his burden' (*TT* I. liv). (He was very aware of how writing something down, too, meant that 'so far from impressing it on the memory we rather disburthen the memory of it'.[10])

By the 1820s he was, though, increasingly vulnerable to the charge of talking for its own sake. It was something of which he was, as usual, well aware; even when young he had known the seductive pleasures of talk. 'O how I wish to be talking, not writing' (*CL* ii. 962), he had impatiently exclaimed in 1803. He not only tended to play 'First Fiddle' in company but 'too often Watchman's Rattle' (*CL* ii. 1022); in 1829, he would cheerfully refer to 'our former Thursday Evening *Conver* – or to mint a more appropriate term, *One*versazioni' (*TT* i. lv). Carlyle, however, believed that Coleridge 'cannot speak; he can only "*tal-k*" (so he names it)' (*TT* i. lviii) and summed up what he suffered in Coleridge's company:

> He is without beginning or middle or end. A round fat oily yet impatient little man, his mind seems totally beyond his own controul; he speaks incessantly, not thinking or imagining or remembering, but combining all these processes into one; as a rich and lazy housewife might mingle her soup and fish and beef and custard into one unspeakable mass and present it trueheartedly to her astonished guests.   (*TT* i. lix)

Their encounter in 1824 made Carlyle exclaim that Coleridge was 'a man of great and useless genius' (*TT* i. lviii); the talk did not *get* anywhere, did not *do* anything. Even aggrieved listeners agreed that Coleridge's talk was 'emphatic' and 'energetic',[11] but Hazlitt would be characteristically savage the following year when describing how Coleridge's faculties 'have gossiped away their time, and gadded about from house to house, as if life's business were to melt the hours in listless talk'.[12] Wordsworth, having spent those weeks with him on the Continent in 1828, also thought that Coleridge's talk 'is now too often dreamy; he rarely comes into contact with popular feelings & modes of thought. You cannot incarnate him for a minute' (*TT* i. xlii). That feeling may even have led Wordsworth to talk more than usual.

The 'table-talk' recorded by several people in Coleridge's later years does, however, allow a limited kind of access to the man Harriet Martineau recalled as being 'gifted or cursed with inordinate reflective and analogical faculties, as well as prodigious word power'.[13] Wordsworth described in 1829, some months after their European tour, what he had experienced:

> S. T. C. never did *converse* in the common sense of the word; he would lay hold of another person's suggestion, & then refine upon it, divide & subtilize it till he had made it entirely his own. He borrowed largely, but he had a right to do so, for he gave away as largely.

And it was expressly while thinking of him as a talker that Wordsworth made his memorable remark that while 'Many men have done wonderful things... S.T.C. is the only wonderful man I ever knew' (*TT* i. xlii). Henry

Nelson Coleridge remarked that the 'habit of his intellect . . . was under a law of discoursing upon all subjects with reference to ideas or ultimate ends' (*TT* I. xliv), and this was what many of his hearers found difficult. It was again, however, what he *believed* in doing; thought it his job to do. He was perfectly able to talk 'on plainer subjects' at times; he could confine himself 'to the detail of facts or . . . spontaneous emotions' (*TT* I. xliv–xlv) when talking to people, sometimes to women, who lacked the advantages of education which Coleridge commonly expected in men.

Recovering his talk, however, is surprisingly difficult. The 'official' table talk entries were cleaned-up by their transcribers, so that Coleridge apparently spoke relatively briefly (most of the transcribed extracts would last only a minute or two if spoken aloud). The speeches are always to the point, too, or they would not have been recorded. Very few accounts provide the sense of the bewildering links, as well as the sheer range, that Keats conveyed in a letter describing his walk with Coleridge in April 1819:

> In those two Miles he broached a thousand things – let me see if I can
> give you a list – Nightingales, Poetry – on Poetical sensation –
> Metaphysics – Different genera and species of Dreams – Nightmare – a
> dream accompanied by a sense of touch – single and double touch[14] – A
> dream related – First and second consciousness – the difference
> explained between will and Volition – so m[an]y metaphysicians from a
> want of smoking [i.e. understanding] the second consciousness –
> Monsters – the Kraken – Mermaids – southey believes in them –
> southeys belief too much diluted – A Ghost story – Good morning – I
> heard his voice as he came towards me – I heard it as he moved away – I
> had heard it all the interval – if it may be called so.[15]

That was most people's experience of Coleridge's talk, and it left them both bewildered and entranced.

However, no other writings in the Coleridge oeuvre, not the published volumes of his table talk, not the marginalia, not even the letters (magnificent though they sometimes are) provide us with such a vivid impression as his late work the *Opus Maximum* and the notebooks of what it must really have been like to hear Coleridge talking. The monologues in his letters rarely convey the sense of his mind spontaneously developing its own thoughts ('My Thoughts crowd each other to death' – *CN* III. 3342) which impressed people so much in live performance. The unedited and convoluted chapters in the *Opus Maximum*, however, authentically bewilder us with the direction they are taking before they start to do what they promised, and the notebooks too offer a good idea of Coleridge's spontaneous and unpremeditated talk; he believed 'I write far more unconscious that I am writing, than in my most earnest modes I *talk*' (*CN* III. 3325).

The notebooks also offer the single voice, speaking on and on, running through a texture of the pertinent, the learned and the incomprehensible, the resigned and the agonised. At times there are natural links between the different subjects but at other times transitions occur where only Coleridge might ever have been conscious of the connections. This was something that listeners to Coleridge's talk very often reported and of which he was (as ever) very aware: 'I skip from one thing to another too fast & unconnectedly' (*TT* I. xlii, 146). A typical notebook entry starts, for example, by discussing the nature of habits as opposed to desires, but develops almost incomprehensibly into a question about the 'marvellous velocity of Thought and Image', segues sideways into a passing consideration of the 'state after death' and the status of desire at that point . . . then takes up the idea of death and declares that the writer cannot look forward to the death of any human being, even though one such death (presumably that of Sarah Coleridge) would free 'all my noblest faculties that must remain fettered during that Being's life'. He believes, however, that to *desire* such a death would itself be 'absolutely suicide, coelicide, not mere viticide',[16] but then returns to an immensely complex hypothetical question (now at last addressed directly to Sara Hutchinson) about how, if he *were* free, 'then, *then*, would you be the remover of my Loneliness, my perpetual Companion?' (*CN* I. 1421).

It seems unlikely that Coleridge began his jottings about habit and desire with any intention of finding his way to framing such a proposal, but as we listen we can hear the subject growing out of the complexities and convolutions of his argument, as his mind oscillates purposefully towards what concerns him most.

In December 1803, again, he started to write summaries of Kant's arguments and to transcribe some extracts (*CN* I. 1705, 1710, 1711, 1717), but other entries began to intrude, including one describing a daydream of being pillowed on a large-breasted woman (*CN* I. 1718). This passage, however, certainly reflects back on Kant, as the transcribed extract which follows shortly afterwards ends with Kant's strictures against the way 'empirical motives' govern human behaviour, and the way that 'human reason in its weariness is glad to rest on this pillow' (*CN* I. 1723). It is exactly as if Coleridge were developing, in the biographical excursus, a very personal if practical application of Kant's propositions. Such, too, must have been his habit when talking.

In such ways, Coleridge's own notebooks remain a guide to the language of his continuing passions and enthusiasms. The penultimate entry in his notebooks, inscribed during the weeks before his death in July 1834, concludes with a magnificent example of a parenthetical sentence which continues for 130 words before launching into a final twenty-eight-word peroration containing the main verb (*CN* v. 6918). Carlyle's brother John, having heard Coleridge talking in 1830, believed 'there is no man in the island puts more thought through himself' (*TT* i. lix). That is a splendid description of the work which filled his best talk and best writing; Coleridge putting thought through himself, as a kind of superlative word processor.

Logic and *Opus Maximum*

From 1816, in the refuge the Gillmans had provided for him, he had at last been able to spend a lot of time on what he had always hoped would be the great work of his life. What he was doing has mostly come down to us in the form of his *Logic* and his *Opus Maximum*. Coleridge always insisted that they were ready for the press when they were a long way from being finished (the *Logic* lacks a promised third part, the *Opus Maximum* is only chapters and fragments). Over the years that followed he continued to read voraciously but also managed to dictate some extended chapters; he was never, however, able to make the progress he had hoped, though the three religious publications of his later years probably creamed off some of the thinking.

The *Logic*, published in full only in 1981, was part of a treatise on connected reasoning which was, in part at least, the product of dictation given to a class of young men which Coleridge apparently conducted between the spring of 1822 and 1823; the treatise was recopied at some point between 1824 and 1827. As has been said, 'most readers of the *Logic* will find that they are indulging in intellectual exercise. But the student of the literary Coleridge is likely to be seeking different game' (*Logic* lxxiii). The same applies to those interested in language and grammar; only the first two 'Introductory' chapters of the *Logic* have much to say directly about language.

The fragments of the *Opus Maximum* were published in 2002. Coleridge's later writings shared a number of themes. They were about language, they were about logic, and they tried to say what was distinctive about being human which led to recovering 'the ideal truth ... of the Christian religion' (*CN* iii. 4440). They attempted to build bridges between the human will, reason and the concept of the *Logos*; Coleridge had insisted for years on 'Christianity the one true Philosophy' (*CL* iii. 533). His ambition had been to identify the links between the ideas of human nature, the theologies, the philosophies and the metaphysics with which he had always been concerned; he wanted to say something of maximum force about Reason, Will and God, and how they necessarily belonged together.

One passage for the *Opus Maximum*, written perhaps in 1832, shows very beautifully two sides of Coleridge: the visionary thinker who wants to link everything up, and the down-to-earth believer typified by the figure of Lieutenant Tom Bowling in Smollett's novel *Roderick Random*:

> Proposed Preface to the first Volume of my Work,
>   the 'Magnum Opus
>   et labor (mea vitae)'
> In my judgement, there are but two schemes worthy the name of
> Religion: and I believe the first is to the Second, as the Acorn to the same
> Acorn expanded into an Oak. The first is that of Lieutenant Bowling – in
> his reply to the Zealous Romish Priest – 'As for me, friend! d'ye see, I
> have no objection to what you say. It may be either true or false for what
> I know. I meddle with nobody's affairs but my own – the Gunner to his
> Linstock [i.e. the long stick holding the lighted match], and the
> Steersman to the helm, as the saying is. I trust to no creed but the
> compass, and do unto every man as I would be done by: so that I defy
> the Devil, the Pope and the Pretender, and hope to be saved as well as
> another.' – The second Scheme the reader will find in the following
> System of Faith and Philosophy: or Catena Veritatem de Deo, Homine
> et Naturâ ['Chain of Truths concerning God, Man and Nature'].
> S. T. Coleridge[17]

Coleridge of course believes in himself as the system-of-faith-creator, the great-oak-schemer, the chain-of-truths-linker; he is not a man of simple, unthinking (if comic) faith like Smollett's Lieutenant. Yet he evinces a deep sympathy, which in its own way may be nostalgic, for such faith.

The problem for the *Logic* and the *Opus Maximum* was not simply Coleridge's inability to finish either work. How *could* a life, a thinking life such as his, manage an all-encompassing statement, torn as he was between a basic religious faith (he believed that life 'begins in its detachment from Nature and is to end in its union with God' – *CM* iii. 919) and the massive, conflicting demands which the sophistication of his thinking and the depths of his knowledge made on him? Christoph Bode may be right in his judgement that Coleridge was 'a great poet and fiction writer, who happened to mistake himself for a profound philosopher',[18] but Coleridge was preoccupied, as Richard Berkeley has said, 'with the attempt to carve out a conception of reason that would somehow combine a determinate rational universe with freedom, consistency with creativity, personality with infinity'.[19] Not being able to bring *that* particular mix to a stable conclusion is perfectly understandable, no matter how energetic his mind or serious his attempts. All he could manage were a series of overlapping arguments around the areas of thought that most concerned him. Hence the fragments that make up so much of his work; and the *Opus Maximum* is, both in detail and at large, especially fragmentary.

The fact that he knew he was drawing to the end of his life may, however, have helped him accept that he was not now going to achieve the very great things he had once set himself to do, and had felt so guilty for not accomplishing. As late as 1816 he had set down his objections to being judged a 'wild eccentric Genius that has published nothing but fragments & splendid Tirades' (*LS* 114 n. 2) and had angrily drawn up a list of what he had achieved. But such things now mattered less. He could now be more content with the fragments, could even conceive of his own work as 'that most religious philosophy which, listening in childlike silence in the outer courts of the temple, blended fragmentary voices from the shrine with the inward words of her own meditation' (*OM* 213). His heart pained him and he also struggled on with the usual stomach problems; he struck Carlyle as 'a fat flabby incurvated personage' in 1824 (*TT* I. lix). Simply being decent and kindly, 'full of religion and affection',[20] reading voraciously as ever, keeping abreast of current affairs, making lengthy notebook entries, being thoughtful for his children (and the Gillman children) so far as he could be without money or a home, and talking wonderfully for the benefit of others and for his own relief – that was all he now set himself to achieve. As he told a friend, 'my Life shuffles by' (*CL* VI. 73), though he remained magnificently funny in anecdote – as when, in 1827, thinking about Andrew Baxter, he recalled how 'in my 24th year I walked with Southey on a desperate hot Summer day from Bath to Bristol with a Goose, 2 Vols of Baxter on the Immortality of the Soul, and the Giblets, in my hand' (*CN* V. 5640). But even at the age of forty-eight, he had felt that 'in *Life* if not in years I am, alas! nearer to 68'; and though he would turn sixty only in 1832, he felt 'a moaning cripple' (*CN* IV. 4606, V. 6891) and looked more like a man of eighty.

Thirty years earlier, about to set off by ship for Malta, he had firmly told himself that 'Death *itself* will be only a Voyage – a Voyage not *from*, but to our native Country' (*CL* II. 1123). That was how he began to feel, with some relief, as his death approached; he no longer wanted to prolong his time in a world in which he had for so long found himself a stranger. He died on 25 July 1834.

Afterword

Coleridge has been fortunate in his admirers. He has been the subject of a hugely praised two-volume biography by Richard Holmes, and in the Bollingen edition of his collected works and notebooks he has been the subject of one of the great scholarly enterprises of the age. Numerous selections of his prose and his poetry are also available.

Coleridge seems to be becoming the archetypal figure of English Romanticism, as individual works of genius become less significant to modern readers. Fragmentary works often have a greater appeal to us than finished ones; a fully worked-out system of philosophy from the 1820s will not interest many people, but Coleridge's fragmentary attempts to create one are fascinating for readers who are happy to believe that the fragments demonstrate 'that he did not regard his philosophy as a closed system, or an ultimate one'.[1] We are also fascinated by the intellectual and political context in which such works appeared, and the philosophical or psychological ideas lying behind them, especially when exemplified in work in non-standard forms (such as Coleridge's notebooks and marginalia). 'Kubla Khan' and 'Christabel' have neither of them suffered from being fragments. If anything, the opposite; opportunities for understanding them can never diminish, their appeal need never fade. And the existence of 'The Ancient Mariner' and 'Dejection' in various versions interests both non-academic and academic readers who prefer to observe process and change rather than to find their reading a source of moral improvement or solace.

The contemporary fascination with biography has also been of enormous benefit to Coleridge's reputation. Modern readers no longer desire to judge him for the failures of his life. On the contrary, they are positively attracted by the addicted, clever, procrastinating, horribly human individual which his biography reveals, and by which his own writing about himself, too, was fascinated. More deeply and consistently than any other writer before the end of the nineteenth century, Coleridge explored his own mental and emotional processes. He believed, he wrote in 1810, in the necessity of giving 'a flesh-and-blood reality' to what interestingly he called the 'processes of the rational and moral Being' which (he knew) were always in danger of becoming 'abstractly intellectual', unable to 'partake . . . of the life and change of material forms' (*CN* III. 3847). Such 'life and change' were central to how he thought and wrote, and to what he thought and wrote about. As poet, translator, critic, essayist, letter-writer, philosopher, religious thinker, psychologist and observer, he straddles the age as does no other English writer. His work was also well known on the continent of Europe; and if he was indeed responsible for the 1821 partial translation of Goethe's *Faust*, he aligned himself precisely beside the other great European polymath of his age.

On the other hand, modern fascination with Coleridge's peculiar achievements can obscure the disappointing nature of some of what he left behind. Scholars who examine the texts, the notes and the fragmentary survivals in the Bollingen edition, and who constantly uncover new depths of learning and analysis, are the last people to admit that Coleridge failed to complete his *Opus Maximum* because he never quite knew what it was about (apart from everything); or that he failed to write much interesting poetry after 1802; or that he allowed his talking to take the place of most forms of written achievement after 1817.

What we can, however, do is view Coleridge's failures as a writer without any need to feel moral about them, or to feel superior to him because of them. We can see them instead as the results of profound ambitions, extraordinary talents, terrible misfortune in his addiction, and a mind interested in almost everything. His preternaturally enquiring intelligence and his verbal precision made him a writer who fascinates every generation anew.

Notes

Preface

1 *The Notebooks of Samuel Taylor Coleridge*, ed. Kathleen Coburn *et al.* 5 vols. (New York, Princeton and London: Princeton University Press and Routledge, 1957–2002), III. 4287. See Jorge Luis Borges, 'The Flower of Coleridge', *Other Inquisitions 1937–1952* (Austin: University of Texas Press, 1965), pp. 10–12, for the coincidence between this entry (itself indebted to the German writer Jean Paul: see *Notebooks* III. 4287 n.), printed for the first time in *Anima Poetae* (London: Heinemann, 1895), p. 282, and the ending of *The Time Machine* (New York: Henry Holt, 1895) by H. G. Wells.

2 *The Friend*, ed. Barbara Rooke, 2 vols. (London and Princeton: Princeton University Press, 1969), II. 17.

3 *Collected Letters of Samuel Taylor Coleridge*, ed. Earl Leslie Griggs, 6 vols. (Oxford and New York: Oxford University Press, 1956–71), 17.

4 Seamus Perry, ed., *Coleridge's Notebooks: A Selection* (Oxford: Oxford University Press, 2002), p. [vii].

5 *Notebooks*, II. 2638, III. 3531.

6 *Ibid.*, III. 3561.

7 *The Letters of William and Dorothy Wordsworth: The Middle Years*, vol. II, part 1, 1806–1811, ed. E. de Selincourt and Mary Moorman (Oxford: Oxford University Press, 1969), 390–1.

8 *Collected Letters*, II. 959.

1 Early life and contexts: 1772–1802

1 Stereotype printing was developed in the 1790s; the 'Claude Lorraine Glass' (first recorded English reference 1789) employs jet, not quicksilver, for its reflection; the 'Camera Obscura' uses lenses to project an image into a darkened room.

2 Rosemary Ashton, *The Life of Samuel Taylor Coleridge* (Oxford: Blackwell, 1996), p. 14.

3 Coleridge's spelling and punctuation, here and elsewhere, have been preserved.

4 *The Collected Letters of Robert Southey, Part I: 1790–1797*, ed. Lynda Pratt, [www.rc.umd.edu/editions/southey_letters/Part_One], Letter 135.

132

5 Thomas Medwin, *Conversations of Lord Byron* (London: Henry Colburn, 1824), pp. 178–9.

6 *The Collected Letters of Robert Southey*, ed. Pratt, Letter 250.

7 *Watchman* 47: cf. Pope's *Rape of the Lock*, III. 18 ('singing, laughing, ogling, and all that').

8 Byron, *Don Juan*, Canto I, xci, and 'Dedication', lines 15–16.

9 See Neil Vickers, 'Coleridge's Abstract Researches', *Samuel Taylor Coleridge and the Sciences of Life*, ed. Nicholas Roe (Oxford: Oxford University Press, 2001), pp. 155–74.

10 James Gillman, *The Life of Samuel Taylor Coleridge* (London: William Pickering, 1838), p. 246.

11 Samuel Crumpe, *An Inquiry Into the Nature and Properties of Opium* (London: G. G. & J. Robinson, 1793), pp. 237, 257.

12 Cf. J. B. Mattison on 'Opium Addiction among Medical Men' (*Medical Record* (29 June 1883), p. 621). As late as the 1860s, however, the dangers of addiction were not understood; they went unmentioned in F. E. Anstie's *Stimulants and Narcotics: Their Mutual Relations* (London: Macmillan & Co., 1864); e.g. Angela Esterhammer, 'The Critic', *The Cambridge Companion to Coleridge*, ed. Lucy Newlyn (Cambridge: Cambridge University Press, 2002), p. 143.

13 Thomas De Quincey, *Confessions of an English Opium Eater*, ed. Alethea Hayter (Harmondsworth: Penguin Books, 1986), 1856 text, pp. 204–5; *CL* III. 475 n. 1.

14 De Quincey, *Confessions of an English Opium Eater*, ed. Hayter, 1822 text, p. 114; the 1856 text would proclaim 'I *did* accomplish my escape' (p. 215); *Samuel Taylor Coleridge: Interviews and Recollections*, ed. Seamus Perry (London: Palgrave, 2000), p. 262.

15 Joseph Cottle, *Reminiscences of Samuel Taylor Coleridge and Robert Southey* (London: Houlston and Stoneman, 1847), p. 38.

16 *CL* III. 513, *CN* II. 3078; *A Memoir of the Life and Writings of the late William Taylor of Norwich*, ed. J. W. Robberds, 2 vols. (London: John Murray, 1843), I. 455.

17 *CN* I. 984; to distinguish Sara Hutchinson ('Asra' to Coleridge) from Coleridge's wife Sarah, I have (like Coleridge at times) spelled the latter with an 'h' (*CN* III. 3826 and n.).

2 Poetry

1 Alethea Hayter, *Opium and the Romantic Imagination* (London: Faber & Faber, 1968), p. 207.

2 See e.g. Malcolm Ware, 'Coleridge's "Spectre Bark": A Slave Ship?', *Philological Quarterly*, 40 (1961), 589–93; Jerome McGann, 'The Meaning of "The Ancient Mariner"', *Critical Inquiry*, 8 (1981), 35–66; Tim Fulford, 'Slavery and superstition in the supernatural poems', *The Cambridge Companion to Coleridge*, ed. Lucy Newlyn (Cambridge: Cambridge University Press, 2002), pp. 45–58.

3 Fulford, 'Slavery and Superstition in the Supernatural Poems', p. 49.

4 *Ibid.*, p. 57.

5 Cf. Coleridge's review of Lewis's *The Monk*: 'wearied with fiends, incomprehensible characters, with shrieks, murders, and subterraneous dungeons, the public will learn ... with how little expense of thought or imagination this species of composition is manufactured' (*SWF* I. 58).

6 Cf. the Duchess of Newcastle declaring in 1656 that she loved her sister with 'a supernatural affection', *The Life of William Cavendish, Duke of Newcastle*, ed. C. H. Firth (London: J. C. Nimmo, 1886), p. 287.

7 Cf. 'when Ideas float in our mind, without any Reflection or regard of the Understanding, it is that which the French call *Resvery*; our Language has scarce a name for it' (John Locke, *An Essay Concerning Human Understanding*, 1690, Book II, xix, 1).

8 William Empson, '"The Ancient Mariner"', *Critical Quarterly*, 6 (1964), 300.

9 *CPI* I. 380, 382. It has been argued that Coleridge had in mind the small, black albatross (*CPI* I. 377 n.; R. A. Foakes, 'Beyond the Visible World', *Romanticism*, 5/1 (1999), 67). Wordsworth had told Coleridge about George Shelvocke's *A Voyage round the World* (1726) and its 'disconsolate black albitross' (p. 75), which *may* have been the Sooty Albatross (*Phoebetria fusca* and *P. palpebrata*, wingspan six feet). But Shelvocke does not distinguish his black albatross from *Diomedea exulans*, which he previously described with a wingspan of 'twelve to thirteen feet' (p. 62); and Wordsworth remembered 'the largest sort of seafowl, some extending their wings 12 or 13 feet' (*The Fenwick Notes of William Wordsworth*, ed. Jared Curtis (London: Bristol Classical Press, 1993), p. 2).

10 In 1804, Coleridge saw sailors shooting at a hawk that had landed on the *Speedwell* far from land; the firing continued when the bird flew to another ship in the convoy (*CN* II. 2090).

11 Coleridge's 1817 gloss makes the problem worse; the sailors 'justify the same, and thus make themselves accomplices in the crime' (*CPI* I. 381).

12 Mary Anne Perkins, 'Religious Thinker', *Cambridge Companion to Coleridge*, ed. Newlyn, p. 188.

13 S. T. Coleridge, *Selected Poetry*, ed. William Empson and David Pirie (London: Carcanet, 1989), p. 242.

14 *Ibid.*, p. 78.

15 Seamus Perry, *Coleridge and the Uses of Division* (Oxford: Clarendon Press, 1999), p. 201.

16 Empson, '"The Ancient Mariner"', p. 318.

17 See Dorothy Wordsworth, *The Continental Journals* (Bristol: Thoemmes Press, 1995), p. 34.

18 John Worthen, *The Gang: Coleridge, the Hutchinsons & the Wordsworths in 1802* (New Haven and London: Yale University Press, 2001), pp. 281–93.

19 Perry, *Coleridge and the Uses of Division*, p. 204.

20 'Prose = words in the best order. Poetry = the best words in the *best* order' (*TT*, I. 90). See too *CN* III. 3286, 3611.

21 See Anya Taylor, *Erotic Coleridge: Women, Love and the Law Against Divorce* (Hound-mills: Palgrave Macmillan, 2005), p. 84.

22 John Beer, 'How Shall we Write the life of Coleridge?', *Samuel Taylor Coleridge and the Sciences of Life*, ed. Nicholas Roe (Oxford: Oxford University Press, 2001), pp. 315–29 (p. 326).

3 Notebooks

1 6,919 entries were identified by Kathleen Coburn, but a number are in the form 1000A, 1000B, etc.; Seamus Perry, 'Introduction', *Coleridge's Notebooks: A Selection* (Oxford: Oxford University Press, 2002), p. [vii].

2 E.g. *CN* III. 4115, *BL* I. 232. Although the 1817 edition ('the only authoritative text' – *BL* I. xix) numbered its chapters in roman, *BL* uses arabic; I have followed 1817.

3 Clement Carlyon, *Early Years and Late Reflections*, 4 vols. (London: Whittaker & Co., 1836–58), I. 29.

4 Mid-life works and contexts: 1803–1814

1 Samuel Crumpe, *An Inquiry Into the Nature and Properties of Opium* (London: G. G. & J. Robinson, 1793), p. 268.

2 MS. 44 at Dove Cottage; William Wordsworth, *Poems in Two Volumes and Other Poems*, ed. Jared Curtis (Ithaca: Cornell University Press, 1983), p. 361.

3 *CN* II. 2373. Cf. *The Life of Brian* (1979, dir. Terry Jones) ending with the crucified Brian and others whistling, singing and toe-tapping 'Always look on the bright side of life'.

4 *CN* III. 3555; the names are enciphered in the original.

5 *Minnow among Tritons: Mrs S. T. Coleridge's Letters*, ed. Stephen Potter (London: Nonesuch Press, 1934), p. 11.

6 *New Letters of Robert Southey*, ed. K. Curry, 2 vols. (New York: Columbia University Press, 1965), II. 117.

5 Language

1 *LL* I. 193. Coleridge had included 'Example of the man at the fall of the Clyde' in his notes (*LL* I. 188) and may have consulted the manuscript of 'Recollections of a Tour made in Scotland' (*Journals of Dorothy Wordsworth*, ed. W. Knight (London: Macmillan & Co., 1897), pp. 191–6).

2 'Recollections of a Tour made in Scotland', p. 195.

3 See Rosemary Ashton, *The Life of Samuel Taylor Coleridge: A Critical Biography* (Oxford: Blackwell, 1996), p. 380.

4 *Samuel Taylor Coleridge: Interviews and Recollections*, ed. Seamus Perry (London: Palgrave, 2000), p. 261.

5 James C. McKusick, *Coleridge's Philosophy of Language* (New Haven and London: Yale University Press, 1986), p. 77.

6 *CN* IV. 4955; Clement Carlyon, *Early Years and Late Reflections*, 4 vols. (London: Whittaker & Co., 1836–58), I. 45; *CN* III. 3762.

7 The second recorded use; see 'with eyes untwinkling' (Robert Andrews, *Eidyllia* (Edinburgh, 1757), p. 24).

8 McKusick, *Coleridge's Philosophy of Language*, pp. 149–50.

9 *CN* I. 1703: 'A genus of unicellular Algæ . . . *Nostoc commune*, formerly believed to be an emanation or deposit from the stars' (*OED*).

10 *CN* III. 4036, 4309. Coleridge did, however, write 'ismium', meaning 'osmium'; he may have been confused by 'iridium', also discovered in 1803.

11 Ashton, *The Life of Samuel Taylor Coleridge*, p. 363.

12 *CN* III. 3160. I have imposed the poetic lineation; the rhythms and rhymes can hardly be coincidental.

13 See James C. McKusick, '"Living Words": Samuel Taylor Coleridge and the Genesis of the *OED*', *Modern Philology*, 90 (August 1992), 1–45.

6 Criticism

1 *Johnson on Shakespeare*, ed. Arthur Sherbo (New Haven and London: Yale University Press, 1968), II. 990, 1011.

2 E.g. *S. T. Coleridge: The Major Works*, ed. H. J. Jackson (London: Oxford University Press, 2000), pp. 640–54, 655–9.

3 *The Fenwick Notes of William Wordsworth*, ed. Jared Curtis (London: Bristol Classical Press, 1993), p. 3.

4 *The Prelude* (1805), VI. 342–5, 329–32.

5 *CPI* I. 142; 'As when heaven's fire / Hath scathed the forest oaks . . .' (*Paradise Lost* I. 613).

6 *Friend* II. 258–9, 147–8; *The Prelude* (1805), I. 428–89, X. 689–727.

7 Clement Carlyon, *Early Years and Late Reflections*, 4 vols. (London: Whittaker & Co., 1836–58), III. 101 n.

8 See *Coleridge: The Critical Heritage*, ed. J. R. de J. Jackson (London: Routledge & Kegan Paul, 1970), pp. 383, 387.

9 *PW* III. 36. Coleridge's phrase had appeared in Robert Southey's *Omniana* in 1812 (*SWF* II, 333–4); see too *BL* I. 293.

10 Or 'esonoplastic' (see *CN* III. 4176), from the Greek 'to shape into one'.

11 Katharine Cooke, *Coleridge* (London: Routledge & Kegan Paul, 1979), p. 93; *BL* I. cxxxii.

12 *Tait's Edinburgh Magazine*, 5 (September–November 1834), 509–20, 588–96, 685–90 and 6 (January 1835), 3–10.

13 Paul Hamilton, 'The Philosopher', *The Cambridge Companion to Coleridge*, ed. Lucy Newlyn (Cambridge: Cambridge University Press, 2002), p. 180; Richard Holmes, *Coleridge: Darker Reflections* (London: HarperCollins, 1998), p. 401.

14 Cf. G. N. G. Orsini, *Coleridge and German Idealism* (Carbondale: Southern Illinois University Press, 1969), pp. 217–19, and Thomas McFarland, *Coleridge and the Pantheist Tradition* (Oxford: Oxford University Press, 1969), pp. 1–52, 256–7.

15 Christoph Bode, 'Coleridge's Philosophy', *The Oxford Handbook of Samuel Taylor Coleridge*, ed. Frederick Burwick (Oxford: Oxford University Press, 2009), p. 603.

16 Hamilton, 'The Philosopher', p. 177.

17 Jonathan Wordsworth, 'The Infinite I AM: Coleridge and the Ascent of Being', *Coleridge's Imagination: Essays in Memory of Pete Laver*, ed. Richard Gravil, Lucy Newlyn and Nicholas Roe (Cambridge: Cambridge University Press, 1986), p. 31; *CN* IV. 5294.

18 Bode, 'Coleridge's Philosophy', p. 608; *CN* IV. 4717.

19 Richard Berkeley, *Coleridge and the Crisis of Reason* (Houndmills: Palgrave Macmillan, 2007), p. 188.

20 Holmes, *Coleridge: Darker Reflections*, p. 254.

7 Later works and contexts: 1815–1834

1 James Gillman, *The Life of Samuel Taylor Coleridge* (London: William Pickering, 1838), p. 131.

2 David Perkins, 'Religious Thinker', *The Cambridge Companion to Coleridge*, ed. Lucy Newlyn (Cambridge: Cambridge University Press, 2002), pp. 190–1.

3 *Coleridge's American Disciples: The Selected Correspondence of James Marsh*, ed. John J. Duffy (Amherst: University of Massachusetts Press, 1973), p. 2.

4 *The Autobiography of Leigh Hunt*, ed. R. Ingpen, 2 vols. (London: Constable, 1903), II. 54.

5 *Faustus, from the German of Goethe, translated by Samuel Taylor Coleridge*, ed. Frederick Burwick and James C. McKusick (Oxford: Clarendon Press, 2007); Roger Paulin, Elinor Shaffer and William St Clair, 'A Gentleman of Literary Eminence', 21 February 2008, http://ies.sas.ac.uk/Publications/stc-faustus-review.pdf

6 *Faustus*, p. 57.

7 'For what are you, my young friend? Are you a beast of the field? No. A bird of the air? No. A fish of the sea or river? No. You are a human boy, my young friend!' (ch. xix).

8 Rosemary Ashton, *The Life of Samuel Taylor Coleridge: A Critical Biography* (Oxford: Blackwell, 1996), p. 348.

9 Clement Carlyon, *Early Years and Late Reflections*, 4 vols. (London: Whittaker & Co., 1836–58), I. 130; *Samuel Taylor Coleridge: Interviews and Recollections*, ed. Seamus Perry (London: Palgrave, 2000), p. 257.

10 *CM* III. 668. Cf. Locke, *Essay Concerning Human Understanding*: 'to disburden the memory of the cumbersome load of particulars' (Book IV, XII. 3).

11 Joseph Cottle, *Reminiscences of Samuel Taylor Coleridge and Robert Southey* (London: Houlston and Stoneman, 1847), pp. 296–7.

12 William Hazlitt, 'Mr. Coleridge', *The Spirit of the Age: or Contemporary Portraits*, 2nd edn (London: Henry Colburn, 1825), p. 71.

13 Harriet Martineau, *Autobiography*, ed. Linda H. Peterson (Toronto: Broadview Press, 2007), p. 302.

14 See *CN* iii. 4046.

15 *Letters of John Keats*, ed. Robert Gittings (Oxford: Oxford University Press, 1970), p. 237.

16 'Coelicide' apparently means 'killing by disembowelling'; by 'viticide' Coleridge probably means 'killing life' (the sense of 'killing vines' is modern).

17 *Roderick Random*, ch. xlii; *OM* 3–4.

18 Christoph Bode, 'Coleridge's Philosophy', *The Oxford Handbook of Samuel Taylor Coleridge*, ed. Frederick Burwick (Oxford: Oxford University Press, 2009), p. 617.

19 Richard Berkeley, *Coleridge and the Crisis of Reason* (Houndmills: Palgrave Macmillan, 2007), p. 210.

20 Ashton, *The Life of Samuel Taylor Coleridge*, p. 367.

Afterword

1 Murray J. Evans, 'Coleridge as Thinker', *The Oxford Handbook of Samuel Taylor Coleridge*, ed. Frederick Burwick (Oxford: Oxford University Press, 2009), p. 340.

Further reading

General reading

Bate, Walter Jackson, *Coleridge* (New York: Macmillan Company, 1968)

Beer, John, 'Coleridge's Afterlife', *The Cambridge Companion to Coleridge*, ed. Lucy Newlyn (Cambridge: Cambridge University Press, 2002), pp. 231–44

Dekker, George, *Coleridge and the Literature of Sensibility* (London: Vision Press, 1978)

Fruman, Norman, 'Coleridge's Rejection of Nature and the Natural Man', *Coleridge's Imagination: Essays in Memory of Pete Laver*, ed. Richard Gravil, Lucy Newlyn and Nicholas Roe (Cambridge: Cambridge University Press, 1986), pp. 69–78

Harding, Anthony John, *Coleridge and the Idea of Love: Aspects of Relationship in Coleridge's Thought and Writing* (Cambridge: Cambridge University Press, 1975)

Levere, Trevor H., *Poetry Realized in Nature: Samuel Taylor Coleridge and Early Nineteenth-Century Science* (Cambridge: Cambridge University Press, 1981)

McFarland, Thomas, 'Coleridge's Anxiety', *Coleridge's Variety: Bicentenary Studies*, ed. John Beer (London: Macmillan, 1974), pp. 134–65

An Oxford Companion to the Romantic Age: British Culture 1776–1832, ed. Iain McCalman (Oxford: Oxford University Press, 1999)

Perry, Seamus, *Coleridge and the Uses of Division* (Oxford: Clarendon Press, 1999)

Vickers, Neil, 'Coleridge's Abstract Researches', *Samuel Taylor Coleridge and the Sciences of Life*, ed. Nicholas Roe (Oxford: Oxford University Press, 2001), pp. 155–74

Wilson, Eric G., 'Coleridge and Science', *The Oxford Handbook of Samuel Taylor Coleridge*, ed. Frederick Burwick (Oxford: Oxford University Press, 2009), pp. 640–58

Biography

Ashton, Rosemary, *The Life of Samuel Taylor Coleridge: A Critical Biography* (Oxford: Blackwell, 1996)

Beer, John, 'How Shall We Write the Life of Coleridge?', *Samuel Taylor Coleridge and the Sciences of Life*, ed. Nicholas Roe (Oxford: Oxford University Press, 2001), pp. 315–29

Holmes, Richard, *Coleridge: Early Visions* (London: Hodder & Stoughton, 1989)
    Coleridge: Darker Reflections (London: HarperCollins, 1998)

Roe, Nicholas, *Wordsworth and Coleridge: The Radical Years* (Oxford: Clarendon Press, 1988)

Vickers, Neil, 'Coleridge's Marriage and Family', *The Oxford Handbook of Samuel Taylor Coleridge*, ed. Frederick Burwick (Oxford: Oxford University Press, 2009), pp. 68–88

Worthen, John, *The Gang: Coleridge, the Hutchinsons and the Wordsworths in 1802* (New Haven and London: Yale University Press, 2001)

Language

Barfield, Owen, 'Coleridge's Enjoyment of Words', *Coleridge's Variety: Bicentenary Studies*, ed. John Beer (London: Macmillan, 1974), pp. 204–18

Coleridge's Writings: Volume 3: On Language, ed. A. C. Goodson (Houndmills: Macmillan 1998)

McKusick, James C., *Coleridge's Philosophy of Language* (New Haven and London: Yale University Press, 1986)

Notebooks

Cheshire, Paul, 'Coleridge's Notebooks', *The Oxford Handbook of Samuel Taylor Coleridge*, ed. Frederick Burwick (Oxford: Oxford University Press, 2009), pp. 288–306

Coburn, Kathleen, *Experience into Thought: Perspectives in the Coleridge Notebooks* (Toronto: Toronto University Press, 1979)

Coleridge's Notebooks: A Selection, ed. Seamus Perry (Oxford: Oxford University Press, 2002)

Ruddick, William, '"As much diversity as the heart that trembles": Coleridge's Notes on the Lakeland Fells', *Coleridge's Imagination: Essays in Memory of Pete Laver*, ed. Richard Gravil, Lucy Newlyn and Nicholas Roe (Cambridge: Cambridge University Press, 1986), pp. 88–101

Poetry

Ebbatson, J. B., 'Coleridge's Mariner and the Rights of Man', *Studies in Romanticism*, 11 (1972), 171–206

Empson, William, '"The Ancient Mariner"', *Critical Quarterly*, 6 (1964), 298–319

Everest, Kelvin, *Coleridge's Secret Ministry: The Context of the Conversation Poems 1795–1798* (Hassocks: Harvester Press, 1979)

Fulford, Tim, 'Slavery and Superstition in the Supernatural Poems', *The Cambridge Companion to Coleridge*, ed. Lucy Newlyn (Cambridge: Cambridge University Press, 2002), pp. 45–58

Gravil, Richard, 'Coleridge and Wordsworth: Collaboration and Criticism from *Salisbury Plain* to *Aids to Reflection*', *The Oxford Handbook of Samuel Taylor Coleridge*, ed. Frederick Burwick (Oxford: Oxford University Press, 2009), pp. 24–48

Lowes, John Livingston, *The Road to Xanadu: A Study in the Ways of the Imagination* (1927; 2nd edn, London: Constable, 1951)

Miller, Christopher R., 'Coleridge and the English Poetic Tradition', *The Oxford Handbook of Samuel Taylor Coleridge*, ed. Frederick Burwick (Oxford: Oxford University Press, 2009), pp. 515–33

O'Neill, Michael, 'Coleridge's Genres', *The Oxford Handbook of Samuel Taylor Coleridge*, ed. Frederick Burwick (Oxford: Oxford University Press, 2009), pp. 375–91

Perkins, David, 'The Ancient Mariner and Its Interpreters: Some Versions of Coleridge', *Modern Language Quarterly*, 57 (1996), 425–48

Richardson, Alan, 'Coleridge and the Dream of an Embodied Mind', *Romanticism*, 5.1 (1999), 1–25

Ware, Malcolm, 'Coleridge's "Spectre-Bark": A Slave Ship?', *Philological Quarterly*, 40 (1961), 589–93

Religion and philosophy

Berkeley, Richard, *Coleridge and the Crisis of Reason* (Houndmills: Palgrave Macmillan, 2007)

Evans, Murray J., 'Coleridge as Thinker: *Logic* and *Opus Maximum*', *The Oxford Handbook of Samuel Taylor Coleridge*, ed. Frederick Burwick (Oxford: Oxford University Press, 2009), pp. 323–41

Hamilton, Paul, *Coleridge and German Philosophy: The Poet in the Land of Logic* (London: Continuum, 2007)

Hedley, Douglas, *Coleridge, Philosophy and Religion: Aids to Reflection and the Mirror of the Spirit* (Cambridge: Cambridge University Press, 2000)

Orsini, G. N. G., *Coleridge and German Idealism* (Carbondale: Southern Illinois University Press, 1969)

Perkins, Mary Anne, 'Religious Thinker', *The Cambridge Companion to Coleridge*, ed. Lucy Newlyn (Cambridge: Cambridge University Press, 2002), pp. 187–99

Wordsworth, Jonathan, 'The Infinite I AM: Coleridge and the Ascent of Being', *Coleridge's Imagination: Essays in Memory of Pete Laver*, ed. Richard Gravil, Lucy Newlyn and Nicholas Roe (Cambridge: Cambridge University Press, 1986), pp. 22–52

Index

Cambridge Introductions to Literature